THE WEB OF BUDDHIST WISDOM

An Introduction to the
Psychology of the Abhidhamma

T0364850

The Web of Buddhist Wisdom

An Introduction to the Psychology of the Abhidhamma

Frits Koster

Silkworm Books

ISBN: 978-616-215-109-5

e-ISBN: 978-1-63102-728-4

English text © 2015 by Frits Koster

All rights reserved

Original Dutch edition was published in 2005

This edition published in 2015 by

Silkworm Books

104/5 M. 7, Chiang Mai–Hot Road, T. Suthep

Chiang Mai 50200 Thailand

P.O. Box 296, Phra Singh Post Office, Chiang Mai 50000

info@silkwormbooks.com

www.silkwormbooks.com

Drawings © 2005 by Fop Smit

Cover: Detail of 'Captured drops' by Joanna Clegg (www.abstractnature.co.uk)

CONTENTS

Part 2: Sublime and supramundane consciousness

Part 3: Mental factors

Part 4: Psychological analyses

Part 5: The body and the experience of enlightenment

ACKNOWLEDGEMENTS

It wasn't easy to write this book, which was first published in Dutch as *Het web van wijsheid* (Asoka 2005). I drew up the framework within a few months, but the subject demanded careful and detailed attention. Fortunately I was able to call on friends with various backgrounds and expertise. They offered their help by reading the manuscript and by giving valuable advice. I would like to express my gratitude to my wife, Jetty Heynekamp, to Khanti Nouwen, Marjó Oosterhoff, Arnica Bosma, Jotika Hermsen, Aukje Rood, Jacob de Boer, Paul Boersma, Gerjan Bozuwa and Herman Zelders for their helpful comments. I also want to express my appreciation for Rob Janssen and Jan de Breet, who gave helpful suggestions regarding the use and translation of Pali terminology. Han de Wit gave me great moral support, and Fop Smit I would like to thank for his playful drawings. Many thanks also to Trasvin Jittidecharak of Silkworm Books, for publishing this English translation of the Dutch original, and to Marjó Oosterhoff for the translation itself.

I also wish to express my respect for and appreciation of my teachers. First of all to the late Venerable Mettavihari, my first meditation teacher, who put me on this path and was always a great source of inspiration. Then to Ajahn Asabha, Sayadaw U Pandita, Sayadaw U Lakkhana and Sayadaw U Kundalabhivamsa. To my Thai *Abhidhamma* teachers, Ajahn Bahnuvat and Ajahn Visud, I offer sincere thanks for their clarity and enthusiasm in explaining the *Abhidhamma* to a Westerner with only limited knowledge of the Thai language.

Finally, I wish to thank my parents for their love for me.

INTRODUCTION

The Web of Buddhist Wisdom is an introduction to the complex teachings of Buddhist psychology, the *Abhidhamma*. It does not aspire to describe all the different facets of the *Abhidhamma*, and it deals only with the first curricula of modern Southeast Asian *Abhidhamma* universities and Buddhist teaching monasteries. Here four ultimate realities (*paramattha-dhammā*) or deeper truths are explored, namely consciousness, mental factors or concomitants, the body or matter, and the experience of enlightenment. These four ultimate realities are the guiding principles of the *Abhidhamma* because they include all experiences we could have as human beings.

Part 1 begins with an introduction to consciousness, from the perspective of Buddhist psychology. Chapter 2 discusses unwholesome types of consciousness (those leading to suffering), while chapter 3 deals with types of consciousness that are not caused by wilful intention and are therefore called 'rootless'. Chapter 4 concludes this part with an analysis of wholesome types of consciousness.

Part 2 introduces forms of consciousness that are not mundane. Chapter 5 and chapter 6 explain fine-material and immaterial types of consciousness, which are related to deep levels of concentration. Chapter 7 takes a look at supramundane forms of consciousness, which are related to the experience of enlightenment.

Part 3 describes mental factors or concomitants of consciousness. Chapter 8 reviews universal and incidental mental factors, and chapter 9 deals with unwholesome concomitants, while chapter 10, chapter 11 and chapter 12 are devoted to wholesome mental factors.

Part 4 refines and deepens the material of the first three parts. Chapter 13 presents two methods of association, namely (1) with

which types of consciousness can the different mental factors
be associated? and (2) by which mental factors can the various
types of consciousness be accompanied? Chapter 14 describes
feelings and root causes, while chapter 15 discusses functions of
consciousness and sense-doors. For the reader who likes to solve
puzzles, part 4 contains some questions; the answers can be found
in the notes.

Part 5 reviews the two last ultimate realities. Chapter 16 deals
with the body and with material phenomena in general, while
chapter 17 shows a model representing our conditioned human
existence. Chapter 18 is devoted to the experience of enlightenment, and chapter 19 discusses the value of the *Abhidhamma* for
modern Westerners.

When reading *The Web of Buddhist Wisdom* some knowledge
of Buddhist teachings is recommended but not strictly necessary.
From time to time I also introduce other themes from Buddhist
psychology, such as the law of cause and effect, the dying process, rebirth, the various realms of existence, the practice of tranquillity and insight meditation, and the four Noble Abodes. In
these 'excursions' I sometimes use information from my previous
books that has been formatted to fit into the framework of the
Abhidhamma. This additional information makes the book accessible to a wider audience.

Because the chapters are closely related to one another I would
advise readers to first go through the book from beginning to
end, and then return to the various chapters and themes to study
them further. The structure of the book also makes it useful as a
work of reference.

The Web of Buddhist Wisdom is aimed at people who are interested in the workings of the mind and who are looking for greater
self-knowledge. May this book contribute to the realisation of
liberating insight.

PREFACE

The history of the *Abhidhamma*

I think that the religion of the future will be a cosmic
religion. Buddhism is the religion that is most compat-
ible with scientific needs.

—Albert Einstein

Buddhism goes back two and a half thousand years. Over time
a great number of schools and traditions have emerged; these
have certain things in common but also show clear distinctions.
The earliest school that is still in existence is *Theravāda* Buddhism,
which is prevalent in Sri Lanka and the Southeast Asian countries
of Thailand, Myanmar (Burma), Laos and Cambodia. The scriptures of *Theravāda* Buddhism can be divided into three categories,
or 'baskets'. The first category, the *Vinaya Piṭaka*, consists of texts
with ethical guidelines concerning the correct behaviour of monks,
nuns and lay followers. The second category, the *Sutta Piṭaka*, consists of the teachings of the Buddha and some of his students. This
category contains the greater part of the scriptures and is very
accessible, so that the theoretical aspects of the Buddhist teachings are easy to understand. The third category, the *Abhidhamma
Piṭaka*, is the most complex set of teachings. *Abhidhamma* literally
means 'higher *Dhamma*' or 'higher teachings', and the study of
Abhidhamma requires a familiarity with Buddhist ideas. However,
when we really go deeply into this material, which initially seems
quite complicated, the *Abhidhamma* offers a surprisingly detailed
analysis of our existence.

The dictionary describes 'psychology' as the science that studies the phenomena of consciousness. In that sense we could say that the Buddha developed a fascinating proto-psychology many centuries before the West began to take an interest in the workings of the mind.

The legendary origins of the *Abhidhamma*

When the Buddha achieved enlightenment, and attained profound wisdom and inner freedom, he initially withdrew into the forests of Northern India. After he carefully studied and reflected on what the experience of inner transformation or *nibbāna* meant to him, the analytical wisdom of the *Abhidhamma* emerged in the fourth week after his enlightenment. According to the *Atthasālinī*, a well-known commentary on the first book of the *Abhidhamma*, the Buddha decided—seven years after his enlightenment—to share his knowledge and wisdom with the beings in one of the heavenly realms, the *Tāvatiṃsa* heaven. His mother had died a week after giving birth to him and had been reborn as a *deva* (divine being) in this heavenly realm. Because his mother had a sharp mind, the Buddha decided to share his teachings with her in an analytical way. Aided by his psychic powers he removed himself to the *Tāvatiṃsa* realm and taught the *Abhidhamma* for a period of three months to a large group of *deva*s under the leadership of his mother, and consequently all of them realised a deep state of enlightenment. In order to sustain his worldly physical body during these teachings, the Buddha returned to earth for a short time every day, and he gave a summary of what he had been teaching in the *Tāvatiṃsa* realm to his disciple the Venerable Sariputta, who was well known for his clear and analytical mind.

The *Abhidhamma Piṭaka*

The Venerable Sariputta elaborated on these teachings and transmitted them to five hundred students, and this is how the foundation of the *Abhidhamma Piṭaka* was laid.

The *Abhidhamma Piṭaka* contains seven books, all written in Pali, the language in which the scriptures of *Theravāda* Buddhism were written down. What follows is a short description of the seven parts of the *Abhidhamma*:

1. The *Dhammasanganī*, or 'Enumeration of Phenomena', consists of a number of schedules (*mātika* in Pali) that contain terms which are used to define and classify all kinds of psychological and philosophical ideas in a manner that is twofold or threefold.[1] These schedules serve as the framework for the whole *Abhidhamma*.

2. The *Vibhanga*, or 'Book of Analysis', describes eighteen explicit themes in Buddhist psychology, like the five aggregates,[2] the four Noble Truths, dependent origination[3] and so on.

3. The *Dhātukathā*, or 'Discourse on Elements', consists of more than one hundred questions and answers about the first two books.

4. The *Puggalapaññatti*, or 'Concepts of Individuals', is the most accessible book, and it defines types of people in various

---

1 Such as 'wholesome, unwholesome and neutral states' or 'with and without roots'.

2 See appendix 1.

3 See chapter 17 for a detailed explanation.

ways, such as 'with a mind like a festering sore, with a mind like a flash of lightning, and with a mind like a diamond'.

5. The *Kathāvatthu*, or 'Points of Controversy', is ascribed to the Venerable Moggaliputta Tissa, an Indian monk who recited this treatise at the third large gathering of the monks (Third Council, around 250 B.C.) as a clarification of philosophical points that were disputed by new schools.

6. The *Yamaka*, or 'Book of Pairs', elaborates on the themes of the first two books. The term *pairs* refers to the consistent dual grouping of questions, like 'Are all *kammi*cally wholesome phenomena wholesome roots? And are all wholesome roots wholesome phenomena?' It is a form of Buddhist logic which is reminiscent of questions like 'Are all sparrows birds? And are all birds sparrows?' The ten chapters in this book are not easy to read, and Mrs. Rhys Davids, an English Pali scholar, called them somewhat plaintively 'the ten valleys of dry bones'.

7. The *Paṭṭhāna*, or 'Book of Conditional Relations', is the most complicated and the most important book of the *Abhidhamma Piṭaka*. It describes the causes and conditions, and the dependent nature, of all mental and physical phenomena. It requires many years of preparation and study to understand this complex work.

Over the centuries many monks have studied these books, and a variety of commentaries have been written. Nowadays the study of *Abhidhamma* involves a monastic training of seven and a half years. Burmese Buddhists in particular have always had a deep affinity with the detailed teachings of the *Abhidhamma*, and consequently many Burmese have detailed knowledge and understanding of Buddhist psychology. I have had the privilege to be allowed to study for some years at the Buddhist university connected with Wat Mahadhatu, one of the largest Buddhist monasteries in Bangkok, Thailand. In this monastery the Burmese method of studying is used to deliver the *Abhidhamma* instruction, and many monks, nuns and lay people get in touch with the profound wisdom of the *Abhidhamma*. The syllabus used is a manual that was written by the Venerable Anuruddha Thera, an Indian monk who lived in the thirteenth century. This manual, which I used as the basis for this book, is called the *Abhidhammattha-Sangaha*: the compendium or manual of *Abhidhamma*. The study involves weekly meetings where the texts are recited in Pali, followed by a translation into Thai. The students use extensive commentaries, reference books and diagrams, then study the texts.

Over the years I have realised how powerful this way of studying can be. When basic texts have been learned by heart they can easily be accessed and used when teaching. Furthermore, the texts are kept alive in this way, and the Buddhist psychology has been transmitted intact from generation to generation for almost twenty-five centuries.

The value of the *Abhidhamma*

Perhaps the *Abhidhamma* cannot be called a science in the modern sense of the word, for it is not based on empirical research in the third person, with sample groups, control groups and so on. Yet Dr. Han F. de Wit, a Dutch psychologist who specialises in religion and is also an author and Dharma teacher, says that the *Abhidhamma* is based on research in the first person, and that it uses the method of 'mental empiricism', as it is called by the methodologist A.D. de Groot. This form of research can be carried out in only the first person singular, but its correctness and actuality can be verified by others. The *Abhidhamma* offers a meticulous description of the 'topography' of profound introspective research by means of the practice of insight meditation, and is therefore called 'contemplative psychology' by Dr. De Wit.

The *Abhidhamma* is phenomenological in nature in that it tries to get to know phenomena in a non-judgemental way as they occur.[4] Because of this approach, many modern scientists have become interested in the old Buddhist descriptions of the workings of the mind, and they are carrying out all kinds of neuro-scientific experiments, for instance into the effects of practising meditation.[5] His Holiness the Dalai Lama, Tibetan Buddhist monk and recipient of the Nobel Peace Prize, encourages this interest wholeheartedly, and he has repeatedly said that if science can prove that one of the teachings of Buddhism is incorrect, that teaching should be adjusted accordingly.

The *Abhidhamma* does not deal with experiences from childhood in a psychological sense, nor does it focus on our everyday problems. It is much more descriptive in nature, and it offers a clear and consistent picture of how human beings function. I call it a transpersonal psychology, in that it gives an extremely detailed description of the human personality. Yet this deeper insight gives us a surprising amount of opportunities for inner growth and freedom. It offers us the possibility of transcending the present personality and it reveals elements that reduce suffering and lead to liberation, which we can realise by means of concentration and insight. In other words: from insight to deeper happiness and a better quality of life.

---

4   The Venerable Nyānaponika Thera, the author of the modern Buddhist classic *The Heart of Buddhist Meditation*, describes the *Abhidhamma* as a 'phenomenological analysis and classification of all experience'.

5   See, for example, *Destructive Emotions* by Daniel Goleman.

The study of the *Abhidhamma* might at first glance seem dry and boring, but when we investigate its subtle structures it turns out to be extremely interesting material. The *Abhidhamma* can be compared to the grammar of a new language we want to learn. We can learn the language by practising to speak it, but it is much easier to grasp if we take the time to study the grammatical structure, which gives us more insight into the logic of the language. The combination of knowing the grammar and practising speaking and reading enables us to become familiar with the language, and we can express ourselves better and more adequately.

The teachings of Buddhism can be viewed as the language of liberating insight. The *Abhidhamma* is the grammar or theoretical structure, while meditation is the direct practical application of and familiarisation with this language. Theory and practice are mutually beneficial and lead to wisdom and inner freedom. On the one hand, the *Abhidhamma* can be the incentive for analytically inclined people to study the Buddhist teachings and through this knowledge begin to practise meditation. On the other hand, the detailed analysis of the many impermanent aspects of body and mind can serve well to deconstruct the concept of a solid and permanent self. This psychological insight can create the space for more flexibility in our lives.

While in Southeast Asia the *Abhidhamma* has become very accessible for ordinary people, up until now only a few readable introductions have been published in the West. This book presents the wisdom of the *Abhidhamma* in everyday English, and it is aimed at psychologists, meditation teachers, meditators and anyone who is interested in the workings of the mind. May *The Web of Buddhist Wisdom* contribute to happiness, peace and wisdom.

PART ONE

MUNDANE CONSCIOUSNESS

Part 1 begins with an introduction to the foundation of the book, namely the four ultimate or indivisible or irreducible realities. Chapter 1 examines the first ultimate reality—consciousness. Chapter 2 discusses unwholesome or unskilful types of consciousness, and chapter 3 describes the so-called rootless types of consciousness. Part 1 concludes with chapter 4, which enumerates the wholesome types of consciousness. All types of consciousness in part 1 are part of our normal everyday functioning.

1

CONSCIOUSNESS

Four ultimate realities

The main purpose of the *Abhidhamma* is to describe and analyse the world—as we know and experience it—as accurately as possible, and by means of this analysis to look for irreducible, indivisible realities in our lives. The *Abhidhamma* distinguishes four ultimate realities (*paramattha-dhammā* in Pali) that are the foundation of the entire *Abhidhamma*. They not only refer to our human personality but also pertain to transpersonal elements that can be realised with concentration and mindfulness. The following four *paramattha-dhammā* are mentioned:

1. Consciousness (*citta*)
2. Mental factors (*cetasika*s)
3. The body or matter (*rūpa*)
4. The experience of enlightenment (*nibbāna*)

The first two realities make up our cognitive and emotional world. The third reality consists of the material world and the body. The fourth reality is supramundane in nature; it is experienced only by people who have extremely subtle powers of observation, which usually requires a long period of spiritual training. The four ultimate realities of our lives are generally taught in *Abhidhamma* universities during the first year of study, and they are the central theme of this book.

Consciousness in Buddhist psychology

In part 1 and part 2 we will consider the first ultimate reality—consciousness. We all have a certain idea about what the term 'consciousness' means, and in order to avoid confusion I would like to start by defining and describing it from the perspective of Buddhist psychology.

In the *Abhidhammattha-Sangaha*, the manual in the study of the *Abhidhamma*, consciousness or *citta* is defined as 'knowing an object'. This knowing is extremely brief; according to Buddhist psychology there are innumerable moments of consciousness in one second. This process can be compared to a television screen: when we watch a programme we do not realise that the screen changes twenty-five times per second, as the screen keeps being built up and is then extinguished. In fact there is a rapid arising and falling away of images, but because of the speed with which this process is happening what we see seems continuous.

The same applies to consciousness: the *Abhidhamma* teaches that in the ultimate sense there is not just one consciousness that is present during the course of the day, but that there are millions of moments of consciousness; all of these have a beginning and an ending, in a relationship of cause and effect. Usually we do not realise that these moments of consciousness are taking place. We may, for example, be lost in thought for long periods of time while thousands of moments of consciousness pass by, but we not are aware of this. From the perspective of Buddhist psychology consciousness should not be confused with awareness. Awareness is being or becoming clearly aware of what is happening in and around us in the present moment. Sometimes we are aware of the *citta*s or types of consciousness that are described in this book, but often we are not aware of them at all. Yet they are taking place, whether we are aware of them or not.[1]

A *citta* knows an object, namely something that consciousness 'delights' in or grasps at. It is a dynamic process that may be compared to an Internet search engine, which traces or finds new websites twenty-four hours a day. There are very many objects a *citta* can be aware of. We can perceive colour and form, sound, smell, taste, hardness, softness, heat, cold, pressure and movement. We can also perceive various mental phenomena like thoughts, ideas, emotions and the experience of enlightenment.

One hundred and twenty-one types of consciousness

The *Abhidhamma* is full of numbers: the three this, the four that, the eight this, the twelve that, and so on. As I mentioned in the introduction, over the years I have come to appreciate this way of storing information more and more. It is a very sophisticated way to commit something to memory, and in transmitting the *Dhamma* (the teachings of the Buddha) the many numbers prove to be of great benefit as an aid to memorising when, for instance, we need to give a lecture. This way of transmitting also means that the essence of the Buddha's teachings has been preserved intact through the centuries, from generation to generation, without losing any of its original meaning. Therefore there will be many lists in this book too.

---

1   Through the practice of insight meditation we can become more aware of the different types of consciousness—see chapter 7 for more information. According to the commentaries, however, only the Buddha was able to recognise all *citta*s in himself.

According to the *Abhidhamma* human beings can experience eighty-nine or one hundred and twenty-one different types of consciousness.[2] These can be divided into four categories:

1. Fifty-four types of sense-sphere consciousness; these are divided into twelve unwholesome, eighteen rootless and twenty-four wholesome types of consciousness
2. Fifteen types of fine-material-sphere consciousness
3. Twelve types of immaterial-sphere consciousness[3]
4. Eight or forty types of supramundane consciousness[4]

Below is a chart with all categories of consciousness (table 1.1).

Table 1.1: One hundred and twenty-one types of consciousness

Twelve unwholesome types of consciousness:

– Eight with desire

– Two with hatred

---

2 See chapter 7 for an explanation of why sometimes eighty-nine and sometimes one hundred and twenty-one types of consciousness are mentioned.

3 The fine-material and immaterial types of consciousness together are called the twenty-seven sublime types of consciousness; they can be realised through the practice of tranquillity meditation. For more details see chapter 5 and chapter 6.

4 Chapter 7 will explain why two ways of counting are used in the supramundane types of consciousness.

- Two with ignorance

Eighteen rootless types of consciousness:

- Seven as a result of unwholesome *kamma*

- Eight as a result of wholesome *kamma*

- Three functional rootless

Twenty-four wholesome types of consciousness:

- Eight active wholesome

- Eight as wholesome effect

- Eight functional wholesome

Twenty-seven sublime types of consciousness:

– Five active fine-material

– Five resultant fine-material

– Five functional fine-material

– Four active immaterial

– Four resultant immaterial

– Four functional immaterial

Forty supramundane types of consciousness:

–   Twenty path-consciousness

–   Twenty fruition-consciousness

How the mind works

Before offering a more detailed discussion of the different types of consciousness, I would like to give a general description of how the mind works. According to the *Abhidhamma* the one hundred and twenty-one different types of consciousness never operate on their own. All types of consciousness in part 1 and part 2 of this book are associated with a number of mental factors or concomitants, called *cetasikas* in Pali. This can be compared to professional football players, who have all kinds of people around them for support: coaches, business managers, physiotherapists, dieticians, fan clubs and perhaps even gurus or spiritual advisors. All these people perform different functions, they all work in the service of the football player, and without these people the players would probably not be very successful in their careers. The football player can be compared to consciousness, while the associates can be compared to the mental factors that accompany consciousness.

Warning

It is important to realise that the one hundred and twenty-one types of consciousness are only part of the mind. Without the mental factors or concomitants, the description of the mind is incomplete. In this book, chapter 2 to chapter 7 will describe the types of consciousness and chapter 9 to chapter 12 will review the mental factors or concomitants. The reader is advised, therefore, not to start searching for the bigger picture immediately; it is better just to read on, and the connections will become clear by themselves.

UNWHOLESOME CONSCIOUSNESS

The previous chapter mentioned four spheres where consciousness can arise, namely in the everyday or mundane sense sphere,
in the fine-material sphere, in the immaterial sphere and in the
supramundane sphere. The first fifty-four types of consciousness from the overview in chapter 1 are mundane types of consciousness, and these occur in the sense sphere. According to
the *Abhidhamma* sense-sphere consciousness can be subdivided
into three categories, which give twelve unwholesome, eighteen
rootless and twenty-four wholesome types of consciousness. This
chapter will discuss the twelve unwholesome types of consciousness (*akusala-cittas*).

Twelve unwholesome types of consciousness

The teachings of the *Abhidhamma* state that when there is
unwholesome consciousness our behaviour is determined by
three unwholesome roots or motives, namely desire, hatred and
ignorance. From these three motives unwholesome activities
arise in our thoughts, speech and actions, such as killing, stealing,
harmful actions in the area of sexuality, lying, gossiping, (inappropriate) rude speech or cursing, speaking nonsense, possessiveness,
ill will or being attached to an incorrect view of reality.

Desire, hatred and ignorance are called unwholesome, unskilful or destructive because they easily cause pain and suffering,

particularly when we cannot deal with them in skilful ways. That is why they are represented by the symbol of a virus. In the first eight types of consciousness desire or attachment is the motivating factor. In the ninth and the tenth type of consciousness hatred is the central factor, and in the last two unwholesome types of consciousness ignorance is the deciding factor.

– Eight with desire

– Two with hatred

– Two with ignorance

Eight with desire

Just as an illness has a cause, so the Buddha concluded that there must be a cause of the suffering we experience, namely desire (*lobha* or *taṇhā* in Pali) and the attachment or clinging (*upādāna*) that usually follows. He mentioned three ways in which this all-consuming force can become obvious.

1. The desire for sense pleasure

By this is meant the desire for and the ensuing attachment with regard to what we see, hear, smell, taste or touch. It is the desire for pleasure, luxury and comfort. As human beings we seem to spend a lot of time satisfying the desire for pleasure. Often one desire has barely been met before we are attracted to the next new sense stimulus. Look, for instance, at the world of commercial advertising, which is mostly concerned with pleasure and sex.

The Buddha never condemned the desire for pleasure, because whether we like it or not it is a driving force that is inherent in life. However, the Buddha did conclude that desire can be the cause of much pain and misery, and that it can be an addictive or blinding force for many people. Desire limits our inner freedom, and satisfaction of the senses is usually very short-lived. Therefore it provides only a limited form of happiness, particularly when we consider how much of our money, time and energy we sometimes invest in obtaining the desired sensual pleasures. Furthermore, sensual impulses can sometimes be so strong that we may (unwittingly) hurt ourselves and others. Sexual desire for a person other than our partner, for example, can result in the break up of a relationship. Unsatisfied desire causes all kinds of frustrations. Sometimes the desire for pleasure can cause enormous or even traumatic problems, as in the case of incest or rape. We also see how people who are addicted to alcohol, drugs or gambling can completely ruin themselves and their families.

These are extreme forms of suffering that largely arise from sensual desire. In fact most people recognise in themselves one or more kinds of addiction or sensual dependency with regard to eating, drinking, cigarettes, coffee, sugar, sex, watching television or surfing the internet.

2. The desire to be or become somebody or something

This second category of desire implies the desire for everything that is more than what we have already. In fact our whole life is permeated with the driving force to live and to become. It is the energy that drives us to satisfy the basic human needs of eating,

drinking, getting enough rest, protection against heat, cold or violence, and earning our livelihood. Examples of this are working
in order to feel self-esteem, the urge to expand, the ambition for a
better or higher position or job, perfectionism, the many and high
demands we make on ourselves and on others, or the desire for
power and influence.

This second form of desire does not need to be condemned
either. One person may be more under its spell than another,
but this tendency is present in all of us. However, if we cannot
deal wisely with this type of craving or desire we may easily
become its victim, often without realising it. Healthy ambition
may change into an extreme form of careerism, which in turn
causes inner tensions. In extreme cases this can lead to neglect-
ing our health, to burnout, or to ethically irresponsible behaviour
towards others.

3. The desire to destroy

This urge too is deeply rooted in our lives and is expressed as the
desire for *not* wanting more or no longer wanting to exist. Examples of this form of desire are not wanting or no longer wanting
to accept physical discomfort, pain, illness, thoughts, sadness,
anger and the like. This urge can also express itself in a negative
self-image and associated actions, or in wanting to end or get rid
of something we acquired at an earlier time. It may be the cause
of inner conflicts, quitting a job or ending a relationship, and it
can even even lead to war, killing or suicide. While the first two
forms of desire are strong forces, sucking us in or overpowering
us, this last force is repulsive in nature and synonymous with
hatred or aversion.

Desire that is not dealt with in a skilful way may easily cause
attachment and thereby limit our freedom and cause frustration,
particularly when the desire is not fulfilled immediately. It turns

out to be an exhausting and in many cases destructive force. In the Buddha's teachings desire is seen as the direct cause for the suffering we experience as human beings.

The term 'unwholesome' (*akusala* in Pali) often leads to confusion. When during an *Abhidhamma* course I used the example of someone who likes chocolate very much, one of the students rightly pointed out that calling this unwholesome consciousness was probably an exaggeration. For here it refers to a harmless form of attachment; we more than likely won't end up in hell just because we enjoy eating something. Yet it is called unwholesome because, if nothing else, it hinders or postpones the experience of deeper happiness.

Therefore I would like to formulate the notion of unwholesome consciousness in the context of the *Abhidhamma* in two ways, namely (1) as consciousness that causes suffering and (2) as consciousness that obstructs and delays both liberation from suffering and the experience of deeper forms of happiness. Examples of consciousness that causes suffering are addictive behaviour and getting stressed or burnt out because unconsciously we try to prove ourselves in our work. Perhaps the term 'greed' is appropriate here. And as an example of the second formulation above we could think of simple sensual pleasures and desires. They are pleasant but they don't give everlasting happiness and we easily get overwhelmed by them. We forget to live wisely, and it becomes more difficult for us to achieve inner freedom and arrive at deeper insights into the nature of life.[1]

What has always struck me in Buddhist psychology is the careful and detailed description of human life, without being

---

1   Because of unawareness or ignorance we usually react to a pleasant feeling automatically with desire and attachment. However, this need not always be so. With wise and careful attention we can instead just be aware of a pleasant or unpleasant feeling without reacting emotionally. See chapter 17 for more details.

judgemental in the sense of 'right' and 'wrong', or 'this is allowed' and 'that is not allowed'. The *Abhidhamma* describes the working of the mind purely in terms of cause and effect, without judgement. In this way the first eight types of consciousness, which are rooted in desire or attachment, are described in the *Abhidhammattha-Sangaha* as follows:

1. One consciousness, unprompted, accompanied by pleasant feeling, associated with wrong view
2. One consciousness, prompted, accompanied by pleasant feeling, associated with wrong view
3. One consciousness, unprompted, accompanied by pleasant feeling, not associated with wrong view
4. One consciousness, prompted, accompanied by pleasant feeling, not associated with wrong view
5. One consciousness, unprompted, accompanied by neutral feeling, associated with wrong view
6. One consciousness, prompted, accompanied by neutral feeling, associated with wrong view
7. One consciousness, unprompted, accompanied by neutral feeling, not associated with wrong view
8. One consciousness, prompted, accompanied by neutral feeling, not associated with wrong view

The meaning of this dry list can be made clearer with an example. The other day I read in the newspaper that employees steal quite a lot of goods from their workplace. Sometimes this happens as fraud, where thousands of euros are embezzled, but more often the theft takes place on a smaller scale, such as when employees take things home from the storeroom. The numbers given to the examples below correspond with the relevant types of consciousness.

1. The first unwholesome type of consciousness: Alfred walks by the supply room of the large company where he works and sees that the door is open. He enters, notices that the storeroom manager is not present, and walks around with curiosity. He comes across new ink cartridges that are the same as the ones he uses for his printer at home. Spontaneously the desire arises in him to take a cartridge home, and with pleasure he puts one in his pocket while he thinks, 'At last some justice. I work so hard for my boss that I am entitled to a reward.'

Explanation: Alfred is not prompted by colleagues or friends; he steals on his own initiative. He experiences a pleasant feeling, and the wrong view expresses itself in the conviction that he is entitled to something that in fact is not his own. Many of the moments of consciousness Alfred experiences during this theft are of the first type.

2. A few months later Alfred and a colleague are in the storeroom looking for new pens for their office. Pleasantly surprised he sees the ink cartridges again. Initially he is a bit hesitant but his colleague encourages him to steal a cartridge. Alfred lets himself be persuaded to steal one; pleased with himself he puts it in his pocket. He is convinced that he is entitled to it, thinking as well that it is a large company and nobody will notice.

Explanation: This time Alfred was prompted or influenced by someone else. In accordance with the teachings of the *Abhidhamma*, prompting or instigation can be brought about by other people but also by external situations or factors.

3. The same situation as with the first type of consciousness, but in this case Alfred is not convinced that he is entitled to the ink cartridge.

Explanation: Deep down he realises that what he is doing is not correct. He could, for example, ask for an ink cartridge or request a pay rise. Yet he cannot resist stealing the ink cartridge.

4. The same situation as with the second type of consciousness, but here too Alfred knows that he is not really entitled to the ink cartridge.

5–8. The same situation as with examples 1 to 4, but here the feeling that is present with the action and the consciousness is not explicitly pleasant but more neutral.

Explanation: According to the *Abhidhamma* sense pleasures or desires are not always accompanied by a pleasant feeling; the feeling can also be neutral. When, for example, I have a cup of coffee, sometimes I can enjoy it immensely but at other times I may be drinking it from habit or attachment, and not explicitly enjoy it. In this last case there is a neutral feeling.

Of these eight types of consciousness, *kammic*ally speaking the first is the most unwholesome and the last type the least unwholesome. With the first type of consciousness we are purely driven by inner impulses, without any external influence. The presence of pleasant feelings also gives more power to the moment and will make the desire or the attachment even stronger. And the presence of wrong view means that we are more uninhibited, so that we are completely clinging to the experience or the situation.

Two with hatred

Hatred (*dosa* in Pali) can be considered the opposite of desire. While desire and attachment are sticky and suck us into an experience or situation, hatred or aversion is destructive and rejecting in nature. Hatred is seen as unwholesome because it is an emotion that is difficult to manage. It can cause much suffering in our own lives as well as in the world at large. Think for example of the many wars and conflicts in and around us, and how difficult it is for conflict mediators to find consensus between the two fighting parties.

Hatred can also be expressed in very subtle ways, such as not accepting pain, illness, or certain thoughts and emotions. This driving force can also show itself in a negative self-image and in actions arising from it, or in wanting to end or destroy something we once gained. It requires a lot of wisdom to deal wisely with hatred or aversion. The next two types of consciousness are rooted in hatred:

1. One consciousness, unprompted, accompanied by unpleasant feeling, associated with hatred
2. One consciousness, prompted, accompanied by unpleasant feeling, associated with hatred

Explanation: There are fewer types of consciousness accompanied by hatred (2) than by desire (8), but the *Abhidhamma* states that it is not correct to conclude that we show less hatred than desire in our lives. According to the Buddhist teachings this completely depends on the person. Some people generate more hatred, while others' lives are more influenced by desire or ignorance. And it is good to realise that the term *dosa* is used as an umbrella term. Types of consciousness with hatred or aversion are, according to Buddhist psychology, always accompanied by an unpleasant feeling, and this feeling also plays an important role when we are complaining or grumbling, or when we are experiencing emotions like jealousy, stinginess, regret, guilt, sadness or fear. When looked at from this perspective we can see that the two types of consciousness with hatred occur quite often. However, in the types of consciousness associated with hatred there are fewer differences in nuance than in the types of consciousness associated with desire, and there are only two possibilities. With consciousness type 9, hatred arises spontaneously, and with type 10 we are prompted by others or by circumstances. In the case of football hooliganism, for example, there are always some people taking the initiative to start a fight. The majority of the people involved usually just let themselves be egged on by the initiators to commit violent actions.[2] And when we suffer a panic attack we usually experience the unprompted type of consciousness with hatred, while a phobia is usually caused by sensitivity to a specific object, like a spider or a mouse.

Two with ignorance

In Buddhism desire and hatred are considered the immediate causes of pain and suffering. In Buddhist psychology another *deeper* cause of human suffering is mentioned, one which prevents us from dealing skilfully with the above-mentioned driving forces. This deeper cause is ignorance (*moha* or *avijjā* in Pali). Sometimes ignorance is expressed as thoughtlessness or as a lack of insight or overview; at other times it shows itself as an incorrect or distorted understanding of reality. In certain situations we may, for example, be fully aware that an action will have unwholesome results, but we cannot help ourselves carrying out this action anyway, against our better judgement. Ignorance does not mean lack of intellectual knowledge. It mainly refers to our not being (clearly)

---

2 Sometimes we may get a kick out of feeling angry. According to the *Abhidhamma* this pleasant feeling is a reaction to the anger; it does not arise simultaneously but just after the consciousness associated with anger.

aware of mental, physical, sensory and emotional experiences, or not interpreting them skilfully. This subtle misunderstanding of reality is not as easily recognised as desire or hatred, but it is nevertheless an invisible dictator behind the scenes that causes all kinds of difficulties. Under the influence of *moha* we do not see clearly what is happening in and around us right now. This means that we cannot deal wisely with desires, attachments and conflicts, so we make errors of judgement.

All this can be compared to computer viruses. When a firewall has not been installed to protect our computer a virus can easily enter and cause our computer to malfunction. However, when we have installed a proper firewall that keeps an eye on the ports that allow access to the computer, this program can detect any virus attempting to enter and problems can be prevented or rectified. In this example the computer is the symbol of human existence and the ports are the six human sense organs: ears, eyes, nose, tongue, body and mind. A computer without virus protection is like living with ignorance, and a computer with a properly installed firewall is like living with mindfulness.[3]

Buddhist psychology states that all problems are ultimately rooted in ignorance, and that ignorance is inherent in all types of consciousness with desire and hatred.[4] According to the *Abhidhamma* there are also two separate types of consciousness where only ignorance is clearly manifest, without aversion or desire. These two types of consciousness are defined as follows:

1. One consciousness, accompanied by neutral feeling, associated with doubt

---

3 This also explains why in the Buddhist teachings the cultivation of mindfulness is given such importance. We will discuss this wholesome mental factor in chapter 7 and chapter 10.

4 See chapter 9 for more details.

2. One consciousness, accompanied by neutral feeling, associated with restlessness

Explanation: These two types of consciousness are accompanied by neutral feeling that is not explicitly pleasant or unpleasant. The eleventh type of consciousness is strongly coloured by doubt or uncertainty; the twelfth and last unwholesome type of consciousness is accompanied by restlessness or nervous agitation. Chapter 9 will discuss these two mental factors.

ROOTLESS TYPES OF CONSCIOUSNESS

According to the *Abhidhamma* a large part of our physical, verbal and mental behaviour is determined by six so-called *hetu*s or 'root causes'. These are the three unwholesome driving forces of desire, hatred and ignorance mentioned in the previous chapter and their three wholesome counterparts in generosity, loving kindness and wisdom. These six roots determine the *kammic* colour of our actions.

EXCURSION: *Kamma*

For clarity's sake I will first give a short explanation of the term *kamma*. This Pali word (Sanskrit: *karma*) literally means 'deed' or 'action', and in Buddhist teachings it points to all physical, verbal and mental activities that are carried out consciously and intentionally. All actions that we do not consciously decide on are therefore not regarded as *kamma*. If we accidentally harm somebody, for instance, then this is not considered a *kammic*ally charged action; if we do it intentionally then it is. Sharon Salzberg writes in her book *A Heart as Wide as the World* that regardless of who acts, the intention or volition behind the act is the *kammic* seed that is being planted. The motivating force behind the action is considered the most important and the most powerful aspect of the action.

In Buddhist philosophy there is no higher power who makes us do things, or to whom we need to justify our actions. We ourselves influence the law of *kamma* by the choices we make, although of course we can let ourselves be influenced by others. As we saw in the previous chapter, what we do after being prompted by others or by external factors has less *kammic* force than if we perform these actions without prompting. The result or fruit of these actions (*vipāka* in Pali) will therefore not be as sweet or as bitter either.

The law of *kamma* can be compared to processes we recognise in nature. A flower grows from a seed; a bee lives on the honey of the flower; and a bear in turn will eat the honey of the bees. In a similar way we as human beings continually experience the dynamics of cause and effect of physical and mental phenomena. When we plant the seed of an apple tree then it will be an apple tree that grows from it, and not a pear tree. This process of causality is determined by the six driving forces or roots that were mentioned at the beginning of this chapter. On the basis of these driving forces we shape our lives and create destructive or constructive *kamma*.[1]

This explanation of *kamma* may make it easier to clarify the meaning of the term 'rootless'. The eighteen types of consciousness without a root cause (*ahetuka-cittas*) are not determined by the above-mentioned six driving forces, and in and of themselves they do not have a *kammic* charge. They are types of consciousness or moments of consciousness that appear and disappear spontaneously; it is impossible for us to give them specific direction. It may be compared with our heartbeat: whether we like it or not,

---

1   More information about *kamma* and its effects is in the next chapter. For a more detailed description of the six roots see chapter 14.

our heart beats without our involvement. The eighteen rootless types of consciousness may be seen as autonomous mental processes. They are depicted as moles, because they dig underground passages in a garden, in between the roots of plants and trees. These passages themselves, however, are free of roots.

– Seven types of consciousness as a result of unwholesome *kamma*

– Eight rootless types of consciousness as a result of wholesome *kamma*

– Three functional rootless types of consciousness

Eighteen rootless types of consciousness

The eighteen rootless types of consciousness are described below:

Seven rootless types of consciousness as a result of unwholesome kamma

1. Eye-consciousness, accompanied by neutral feeling
2. Ear-consciousness, accompanied by neutral feeling
3. Nose-consciousness, accompanied by neutral feeling
4. Tongue-consciousness, accompanied by neutral feeling
5. Body-consciousness, accompanied by unpleasant feeling

6. Receiving-consciousness, accompanied by neutral feeling
7. Investigating-consciousness, accompanied by neutral feeling

Eight rootless types of consciousness as a result of wholesome kamma

1. Eye-consciousness, accompanied by neutral feeling
2. Ear-consciousness, accompanied by neutral feeling
3. Nose-consciousness, accompanied by neutral feeling
4. Tongue-consciousness, accompanied by neutral feeling
5. Body-consciousness, accompanied by pleasant feeling
6. Receiving-consciousness, accompanied by neutral feeling
7. Investigating-consciousness, accompanied by neutral feeling
8. Investigating-consciousness, accompanied by pleasant feeling

Three functional rootless types of consciousness

1. Five-sense-door-adverting-consciousness, accompanied by neutral feeling
2. Mind-door-adverting-consciousness, accompanied by neutral feeling
3. Smile-producing-consciousness, accompanied by pleasant feeling

All these eighteen kinds of consciousness take place without a *kammic* driving force. They happen to us without any effort on our part. But they *can* be the result of a previously performed *kamma*. This can be compared to sowing grain. Sowing is an act of will; the growth of the seed and appearance of the plant happen as the natural consequences. In Buddhist psychology it is said that the first seven rootless types of consciousness take place as the result of previously performed *kamma* that was influenced by the three forces that increase human suffering or that hinder deeper happiness, namely desire, hatred and ignorance. The next eight rootless types of consciousness happen as the effect of previously performed *kamma* that is slightly wholesome in character.[2] The last three rootless types of consciousness, which will be discussed at the end of this chapter, are neither cause nor effect but are purely functional.

EXCURSION: Cognitive processes

For clarity's sake it might be better to explain first what happens in our minds during a cognitive process. The *Abhidhamma* analyses this process in a very detailed way as seventeen different moments of consciousness. This process, which happens extremely quickly, is illustrated below in table 3.1.

Table 3.1

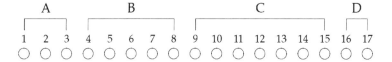

Phase A: Passive state of rest

1. The passive mental state, when no object is received (*atita-bhavanga*)
2. The first impulse in that passive state of mind (*calana-bhavanga*)

---

2 If previous actions were extremely wholesome, the eight wholesome resultant types of consciousness mentioned in chapter 4 would be the result.

3. The passive state is disrupted (*bhavaṅgupaccheda*)

Explanation: The cognitive process starts with a passive state of mind in which no clear objects are experienced. This passive state, depicted as phase A in the model above, does not take place only at night but also during the day, in between all the stimuli we experience. This state is called *bhavaṅga*, usually translated as 'life-continuum' or 'basic current of existence'. Perhaps it is best to leave this term untranslated. Different resultant or *vipāka* types of consciousness can perform the function of *bhavaṅga*.[3] The first three moments of consciousness in this process of cognizing an object at the sense-doors take place in *bhavaṅga*.

Phase B: Perceiving the object

4. The mind turns to an object that is perceived through one of the five sense-doors (*pañcadvāravajjana-citta*)
5. Sense-consciousness arises (*pañcaviññāṇa-citta*)
6. The object is received clearly (*sampaṭicchana-citta*)
7. The received object is investigated (*santīrana-citta*)
8. The determining of the object takes place (*votthapana-citta*)

Explanation: During phase B of the cognitive process we perceive an object through one of the five sense-doors. This object becomes increasingly clear to us. We have no choice in this; it just happens to us. The second phase ends with mind-door-adverting-consciousness that performs the function of determining or deciding. This type of consciousness decides how we interpret the sense object in emotional terms.

---

3 For more details of the different functions see chapter 15.

Phase C: Interpretation

9–15. In these moments the so-called mental scanning takes place by way of seven wholesome or unwholesome types of consciousness that interpret or judge. They perform the function of *javana* or 'mental impulse'.

Explanation: During phase C, mental choices and free will come into play. When the object has been received and determined with careful attention, we interpret the perceived object in a wholesome way. When there has been careless or unwise attention, we judge the object in an unwholesome way. In this phase an emotional reaction arises: types of consciousness 'run through the object' and scan the object emotionally. The first eight moments take place without us having any choice in the matter and therefore they are passive in nature. In the third phase an active mental or emotional judgement takes place or an interpretation happens in the form of anger, friendliness, fear, enjoyment and so on.

Phase D: Registration and return

16–17. Registering-consciousness (*tadālambana-* or *tadārammaṇa-cittas*). Here the experience is stored in the subconscious memory; these moments take place again in the life-continuum, the *bhavaṅga-sota*.

Explanation: Eventually the experience is stored in the subconscious memory during phase D with two registering type of consciousness. When both the sense stimulus and the emotional interpretation of it have finished we always return to the *bhavaṅga*. From this undercurrent of consciousness or life-continuum, new impulses or stimuli will be experienced—an inner movement comparable to the workings of our heart, which from a state of rest makes pumping movements over and over again and then comes back to rest.

As we saw in chapter 1, most of the time we are not aware or barely aware of these cognitive processes because they happen so quickly. According to the commentaries even the Venerable Sariputta, who was known as the most intelligent student of the Buddha, could not distinguish all the different types of consciousness in a cognitive process in himself. In order to make it more understandable the traditional *Abhidhamma* teachers illustrate the cognitive process with a story; I have added in parentheses the types of consciousness corresponding with table 3.1.

A man is taking a nap under a mango tree (1–3). Suddenly a ripe mango falls down and lands right next to his ear. The sound wakes him up (4), he opens his eyes and looks around (5). He then reaches out and picks the mango up (6). He peels the mango (7) and smells it (8). Next he eats the mango (9–15), tastes it (16–17) and resumes his nap.

The possibility for change

The above-mentioned process happens extremely fast; in fact it happens so quickly that we are usually able to distinguish only a few types of consciousness. Nevertheless this analysis offers, in my view, a wonderful insight into the workings of our mind, and it also offers valuable opportunities for change. We continually experience sense stimuli, and we cannot block ourselves off from them. Even in a fully insulated room we will still hear our heartbeat and feel the contact of the feet with the floor; even in the quietest place on earth we experience emotions. Usually we are not aware or barely aware of the stimuli and the emotions we experience. According to Buddhist psychology, however, we can also ensure that we have a subtle, careful attention, so that we are not automatically conditioned by the stimuli we experience.

As a case in point, what follows is the description of a day in the life of Susan, who works as a personal assistant in a large company. All day long she receives stimuli. Her assignment for today is to finish the annual report. But her boss keeps asking her to do certain other quick tasks, colleagues email her with all kinds of questions about the company, she has to take minutes at a meeting, and she needs to make sure that someone collects her sick child from play school. At last she gets time to work on the annual report, and with concentration she starts doing so. Suddenly the phone rings. Because she is concentrating deeply on her work, Susan tries to ignore the ringing phone. So she gives unwise attention to these sounds. Actually, these sounds disturb her and therefore, as an automatic reflex, scanning moments of consciousness with irritation arise. The result is that she can no longer concentrate on the report and she ends up being annoyed with 'those terrible people who keep pestering her'. With wise attention, which means non-judgemental attention, she could have perceived the sounds for what they are and just have waited until the answering machine kicked in.

In Buddhist psychology it is said that we have many opportunities for change, and that we can liberate ourselves from our inflexible habitual patterns. This shows at the same time the appreciation Buddhism has for the development of mindfulness or open awareness. For when we are aware of sense stimuli, and of our inner world in general, we are far less conditioned by unwholesome types of consciousness. Slowly but surely we can liberate ourselves from the power of afflictive emotions like desire, aversion and ignorance. Mindfulness and mindfulness training will be introduced in chapter 7.

Seven rootless types of consciousness as a result of unwholesome *kamma*

The first five of the first seven rootless (*ahetuka*) types of consciousness refer to the fifth moment in the cognitive process. These are the everyday experiences of seeing, hearing, smelling, tasting and touching. These moments of consciousness are very basic. Only at a later stage do we properly recognise what we see, and only then are we really judging the object as beautiful, ugly, and so on. Because these moments of sense-consciousness have very little power—they just happen to us—the first four types of consciousness are accompanied by neutral feeling. As a result of previous unwholesome *kamma* the object we see, hear, smell or taste is somewhat unpleasant in nature. Because the body is a much coarser sense organ than the other four, the subtle neutral feeling is not experienced and the feeling is unpleasant in nature.

The sixth type of consciousness is the sixth moment in the cognitive process: receiving-consciousness accompanied by neutral feeling. In this case the primary sense stimulus is somewhat more clearly perceived.

The seventh type of consciousness refers to the seventh moment in the cognitive process. The object that was just received is now being investigated: What is it? What is happening? All these moments of consciousness are arising and passing away in a process of cause and effect that happens extremely rapidly—so quickly, in fact, that we are usually not aware of it. Here too we don't have any choice in the matter; these processes happen as a natural or autonomous mechanism.

Eight rootless types of consciousness as a result of wholesome *kamma*

The first four of the eight rootless types of consciousness as the result of previous wholesome *kamma* are identical to the first four of the seven rootless types of consciousness as a result of unwholesome *kamma*. These types of sense-consciousness (seeing, hearing, smelling and tasting) too are accompanied by neutral feeling. They are slightly pleasant, however, because the object is more pleasant in nature. The fifth type of sense-consciousness, body-consciousness, is accompanied by pleasant feeling because of its coarser nature.

The next type of consciousness without root cause is again a receiving-consciousness and is identical with the sixth type of consciousness of the first list.

When the cognized and received object makes a strong impression and feels explicitly pleasant, the seventh type of consciousness arises: investigating-consciousness accompanied by pleasant feeling. When the received object makes an impression that is not as strong, the investigating-consciousness that arises is neutral.

Three functional rootless types of consciousness

The first type of consciousness in this third category shows itself during the fourth moment in the cognitive process and is called *pañcadvāravajjana-citta* in Pali, which can be translated as 'consciousness that is adverted to one of the five sense-doors'. These doors refer to the five sense organs: the eyes, the ears, the nose, the tongue and the body.

The second type of consciousness is traditionally called *manodvāravajjana-citta* or 'consciousness that is adverted to the mind-door'; it gives access to thought.[4] This type of consciousness can be expressed in two ways. First of all it manifests—in the function of determining—as the eighth moment of consciousness in the cognitive process. But this *citta* also arises when there is a mind-door process, as a variant of the sense-door processes.

EXCURSION: Mind-door processes
••
Table 3.2

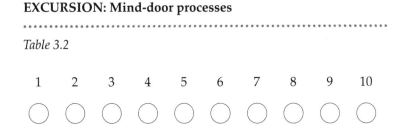

1. In the *Abhidhamma* the subconscious stream of consciousness, *bhavaṅga*, is considered the stepping stone to mental perception processes. The *bhavaṅga* is interrupted at number 1 by a *manod-vāravajjana-citta*, a 'moment of consciousness that is adverting to the mind-door'.

2–8. At numbers 2 to 8 seven wholesome or unwholesome types of consciousness arise. Just as with numbers 9 to 15 in the sense-door process, it concerns types of consciousness that have a scanning function and that interpret and judge the object mentally or emotionally. It is good to realise that the *javana-citta*s in a sense-door process are invariably in the service of the sensory object; therefore they are always related to the sense stimulus that is experienced in that moment. The object of the scanning types

---

4   Chapter 14 gives more information about the six doors.

of consciousness in a mind-door process too can be sensory in nature; for example when we are still enjoying something we saw or smelled. But the *javana-citta*s in a mind-door process can also be linked to another thought object that is completely unrelated to seeing, hearing, smelling, tasting and touching, and that happened in the past, the present or the future, or to an object that is timeless.[5]

9–10. The mind-door process ends again with two moments of registering-consciousness.

....

The smile of the *arahat*

The last rootless type of consciousness is somewhat strange. Whereas the first seventeen *ahetuka-citta*s are experienced by all people in their everyday existence, the last type of consciousness can be experienced only by *arahat*s, people who through long spiritual training have realised the highest stage of enlightenment and who have completely purified their mind from desire, hatred and ignorance.[6]

According to the *Abhidhammattha-Sangaha* several forms of consciousness can happen when we smile. All moments of smiling are accompanied by pleasant feeling. We may smile with one of the first four unwholesome types of consciousness, where desire and attachment are predominant. When we smilingly enjoy looking at a beautiful man or woman we can experience these types of

---

5 'Timeless objects' in the context of the *Abhidhamma* refer to concepts and to the experience of enlightenment.

6 A detailed explanation of the enlightenment experience and 'those whose mind is completely purified' can be found in chapter 7 and chapter 18.

consciousness. We can also smile with one of the first four wholesome types of consciousness—which will be reviewed in the next chapter—and experience pleasure or happiness when we commit an act of generosity, for example. An *arahat* no longer creates *kamma* because his or her mind has been completely purified; their actions have become purely *kriyā* or functional. When an *arahat* smiles, he or she will do so with one of the first four wholesome functional *citta*s or with the last rootless type of consciousness, which is called *hasituppāda-citta*, or 'smile-producing-consciousness'. It is described as a subtle and spontaneous joyful smile, arising from the understanding that suffering—caused by desire, hatred and delusion—has been ended.

According to Buddhist psychology we can smile or laugh in six ways. The first form is the subtlest. It is a smile that is shown only in the facial expression; a smile like that of the Mona Lisa. The *hasituppāda-citta* is an example of this. In the next stage the smile is accompanied by a slight tremor of the lips, just enough to show something of the teeth. Then we may make a laughing sound, and in the fourth stage the laugh is accompanied by movements of the head, the shoulders and the arms. In the fifth stage we laugh with tears running down our face, and in the strongest variant we burst out laughing, moving backwards and forwards with the whole body. On this joyful note we have come to the end of the explanation of the eighteen rootless types of consciousness.

4

WHOLESOME CONSCIOUSNESS

The third group of mundane types of consciousness consists of twenty-four wholesome types of consciousness: the so-called *sobhana-citta*s (literally, 'beautiful' types of consciousness). These *citta*s lighten our suffering and contribute to the experience of happiness, peace and harmony. Therefore they are sometimes called 'great' (*mahā*). In the drawing below they are depicted as elephants, because in Asia it is said that these great animals bring happiness and prosperity. With these *citta*s our lives are conditioned by the opposites of the three unwholesome driving forces mentioned in chapter 2. Generosity, loving kindness and wisdom—or even just the absence of desire, hatred and ignorance— are now centre stage in our thoughts, speech and actions. The twenty-four wholesome types of consciousness can be divided into three groups, which are depicted below.

– Eight active wholesome types of consciousness

– Eight types of consciousness as a result of wholesome *kamma*

–   Eight functional wholesome types of consciousness

Eight active wholesome types of consciousness

The first eight 'beautiful' types of consciousness, also called *kāmāvacara-kusala-cittas*, are *cittas* that arise when we create wholesome *kamma*. It concerns actions that are motivated by generosity, loving kindness and insight or wisdom. In this context a list of ten wholesome actions are mentioned:

1. Practising generosity
2. Following a code of ethics that promotes harmony
3. Practising meditation
4. Dealing respectfully with ourselves and with others
5. Being of service to others, being altruistic
6. Sharing merit with others
7. Rejoicing in the happiness and good fortune of others
8. Reading about, listening to and discussing topics that promote harmony and wisdom
9. Explaining the *Dhamma*
10. Rectifying incorrect views in ourselves—which means views or opinions that cause suffering

The first eight 'beautiful' types of consciousness are defined as follows:

1. One consciousness, unprompted, accompanied by pleasant feeling, associated with wisdom

2. One consciousness, prompted, accompanied by pleasant feeling, associated with wisdom
3. One consciousness, unprompted, accompanied by pleasant feeling, not associated with wisdom
4. One consciousness, prompted, accompanied by pleasant feeling, not associated with wisdom
5. One consciousness, unprompted, accompanied by neutral feeling, associated with wisdom
6. One consciousness, prompted, accompanied by neutral feeling, associated with wisdom
7. One consciousness, unprompted, accompanied by neutral feeling, not associated with wisdom
8. One consciousness, prompted, accompanied by neutral feeling, not associated with wisdom

Just as with the first eight unwholesome or *akusala* forms of consciousness discussed in chapter 2, the first four wholesome types of consciousness mentioned above are accompanied by pleasant feeling, while the last four are accompanied by neutral feeling. There is also a division based on whether they are being prompted or unprompted. Finally, four of the eight wholesome types of consciousness are associated with wisdom, while the other four take place without the presence of wisdom. Some examples to explain the above:

1. With the first type of consciousness there is the spontaneous idea to support a charity that helps people who have been affected by famine. We experience a pleasant, satisfied feeling and realise that our contribution will be beneficial for the happiness and well-being of many.

2. With the second wholesome type of consciousness we are watching television and see a moving documentary about all the

suffering that is caused by famine and drought. Touched by this documentary we decide to give a donation. We feel good about having decided to do so and we realise that this act of compassion and generosity will bear fruit.

3. With the third 'beautiful' type of consciousness the idea to help someone arises spontaneously. We enjoy doing so but do not really have the understanding that it is beneficial and why. We do it only because it makes us feel good.

4. With the fourth type of consciousness we are again influenced by a television programme, or by someone else who is talking enthusiastically about a charity; we let ourselves be persuaded to support this worthy cause. We feel good about it, but here too we do something without realising why it is good to act in this way.

5–8. The fifth to the eighth wholesome types of consciousness are similar to the first four types of consciousness. Only now they are not accompanied by a pleasant feeling but by a neutral feeling. According to the *Abhidhamma* the first wholesome type of consciousness is *kammic*ally speaking the most powerful, and the eighth type of consciousness is the weakest.

Performing wholesome *kamma* is an art in itself and as the saying goes, 'Practice makes perfect.' Fortunately the Buddha gave a number of guidelines to perfect this art. We can make sure that the environment is suitable to perform wholesome *kamma*, for example by choosing a job or a pastime where we don't cause harm and where we can be of service. It is also advisable to create a social network consisting of wise and encouraging friends. Furthermore we can 'polish ourselves' by means of study and meditation so that we can more easily perform wholesome *kamma*. Finally, cultivating actions in body, speech and mind that promote well-being and harmony can help to get in touch with this wholesome stream of life in the future.

Eight types of consciousness as a result of wholesome *kamma*

The ninth to sixteenth types of consciousness are passive *citta*s that arise spontaneously as a result of previously performed wholesome actions. It is no longer necessary to do anything to create this wholesome *kamma*. These *citta*s arise by themselves, just like a plant that emerges naturally from a seed we planted. They are defined as follows:

1. One consciousness, unprompted, accompanied by pleasant feeling, associated with wisdom
2. One consciousness, prompted, accompanied by pleasant feeling, associated with wisdom
3. One consciousness, unprompted, accompanied by pleasant feeling, not associated with wisdom
4. One consciousness, prompted, accompanied by pleasant feeling, not associated with wisdom
5. One consciousness, unprompted, accompanied by neutral feeling, associated with wisdom
6. One consciousness, prompted, accompanied by neutral feeling, associated with wisdom
7. One consciousness, unprompted, accompanied by neutral feeling, not associated with wisdom
8. One consciousness, prompted, accompanied by neutral feeling, not associated with wisdom

These correspond to the eight wholesome types of consciousness. The *Abhidhamma* states that these *citta*s are the result of wholesome types of consciousness from previous lives. They perform the function of rebirth consciousness and can be found in the function of *bhavaṅga* in people and in divine beings. They also arise when a wholesome activity is registered and stored in memory. Finally they can play a role as death-consciousness.[1]

EXCURSION: The process of dying

The term 'rebirth' is often connected with the law of *kamma* as it was described in the previous chapter. The principle of *kamma* operates like a continuation of energy, namely the perpetuation of what is called 'the cycle of rebirth' (*samsāra*). It is presumed that we are not born as a *tabula rasa*, a clean slate, but that there is a *kammic* store of experiences and conditionings from previous lives. According to Buddhism life does not completely end at death, but a transfer of energy takes place to the next life.

First of all, what happens when death occurs? The *Abhidhamma* gives a very detailed answer to this question. It states that death indicates the end of the present existence and that all mental and physical processes end. When we are dying—whatever the cause of our death may be—a rather strange process of consciousness precedes death consciousness. This process is illustrated below.

Table 4.1

	A			B			C				D		E
1	2	3	4	5	6	7	8	9	10	11	12

$\bigcirc \quad \bigcirc \quad \bigcirc \quad \bigcirc \quad \bigcirc \quad \bigcirc \quad \bigcirc \quad \bigcirc \quad \bigcirc \quad \bigcirc \quad \bigcirc \quad \bigcirc$

---

1   See chapter 3: the first three (*bhavaṅga*) types of consciousness in the cognitive processes.

1–3. The first three moments (phase A) are the same as those of a sense-door process. First of all there is the passive state of consciousness, *bhavaṅga*, when no objects are received. This state is disturbed and subsequently interrupted. The first three moments take place in the *bhavaṅga*.

4. In phase B a mind-door adverting consciousness (*manodvārā-vajjana-citta*) occurs.

5–9. From the fifth to the ninth moment of consciousness in phase C 'mentally scanning types of consciousness' (*javana-cittas*) occur—similar to the sense-door and mind-door processes. Just before death the energy begins to weaken, and therefore only five scanning moments take place instead of the usual seven. The content or the object of mental scanning is also different from usual, and there are three possibilities:

A.   A so-called *kamma* presents itself through the mind-door. This is an action that was done previously in this life, or sometimes it is an action done in the present with a strong *kammic* charge. Examples of this are special or frequent acts of generosity, compassion or cruelty.

B.   A *kamma-nimitta* presents itself. This is an object that is perceived through the senses and manifests as a symbol of a previously committed act, as mentioned in (a). Examples of a *kamma-nimitta* are seeing the happy face of the person we helped, seeing blood if we have been fighting, or smelling incense if we spent much time in church or at the temple.

C.   A *gati-nimitta* may appear. This refers to a vision that gives an impression or is a symbol of a future life. In this case we may see images like those from the paintings of Hieronymus Bosch, or we might see beautiful heavenly images.

10–11. Registering-consciousness (*tadārammaṇa-citta*) occurs. In phase D the experience from the *javana*s is stored in the subconscious.

12. This is the actual moment of dying, called *cuti-citta*. In phase E the present life is completely ended.

When people ask me whether this really happens when we die, I usually answer as follows: 'I hope to experience this consciously when the time comes, and only then can I verify this.' In any case it seems a plausible theory. It might explain why my grandmother saw a heavenly gate just before she died, and why others may be fearful or confused when they are in the process of dying.

....

Eight functional wholesome types of consciousness

Finally, a third group mentions eight functional wholesome types of consciousness or *kāmāvacara-kriyā-citta*s. These are experienced only by *arahat*s, instead of the first eight wholesome *citta*s. The reason for this I have already described in the previous chapter. *Arahat*s no longer act in ways that have *kammic* consequences, and they do not experience rebirth after they die. Although they are not always fully conscious of their actions and therefore sometimes perform actions that are not accompanied by insight, any such actions are always free of harmful charge. The mental states of an *arahat* are totally 'clean' but not always filled with insight. There is a story about the Venerable Sariputta, who from pure delight in the *Dhamma* spontaneously started to jump up and down without being aware of what he was doing in that moment.

The last eight wholesome types of consciousness are defined as follows:

1. One consciousness, unprompted, accompanied by pleasant feeling, associated with wisdom
2. One consciousness, prompted, accompanied by pleasant feeling, associated with wisdom
3. One consciousness, unprompted, accompanied by pleasant feeling, not associated with wisdom
4. One consciousness, prompted, accompanied by pleasant feeling, not associated with wisdom
5. One consciousness, unprompted, accompanied by neutral feeling, associated with wisdom
6. One consciousness, prompted, accompanied by neutral feeling, associated with wisdom
7. One consciousness, unprompted, accompanied by neutral feeling, not associated with wisdom
8. One consciousness, prompted, accompanied by neutral feeling, not associated with wisdom

The twelve unwholesome, the eighteen rootless and the twenty-four wholesome types of consciousness described so far are collectively called the fifty-four types of consciousness of the sense sphere (*kāmāvacara-citta*s).

PART TWO

SUBLIME AND SUPRAMUNDANE CONSCIOUSNESS

The types of consciousness described in part 1 concern our everyday lives. The types discussed in part 2 are exclusive; they are not experienced by everyone. The *citta*s in chapter 5 are fine-material in nature; those in chapter 6 go beyond the fine-material level and are immaterial in nature. The fine-material and immaterial types of consciousness can only be experienced through the practice of tranquillity meditation; they are also called 'sublime' or 'expanded'. The types of consciousness described in chapter 7 are supramundane (*lokuttara*) in nature. They go beyond conditioned existence and can be experienced through the practice of insight meditation. They also form the highest goal that can be realised in meditation and have an extremely purifying influence on our mind.

5

FINE-MATERIAL TYPES OF CONSCIOUSNESS

As I indicated in the introduction to part 2, the types of consciousness I will be discussing in this chapter and the next are not mundane, and they can be experienced only through the practice of tranquillity meditation. Because they are extremely blissful in nature they are also called 'sublime', 'expanded' or 'extremely great' (*mahaggata*). They are depicted as butterflies that can flutter around peacefully on a sunny day. As they are connected with the practice of tranquillity meditation, I will first of all give a short description of this type of meditation.

EXCURSION: Tranquillity meditation

In Buddhism, meditation is seen as the most effective way to attain profound peace and wisdom, and to reach the end of suffering. If we really want to understand the Buddha's teachings, practising meditation is essential. Dictionaries typically describe it as religious reflection or contemplation, but this description does not fully cover what the Buddha meant. In Pali the term generally used for meditation is *bhāvanā*, which can be translated as 'cultivating or developing the mind'. So it implies a training process. Just as we go to the gym to increase our physical fitness and stamina, in (Buddhist) meditation techniques we develop wholesome mental powers like mindfulness and concentration. Generally speaking, two main types of meditation can be distinguished:

tranquillity meditation (*samatha-bhāvanā*) and insight meditation (*vipassanā-bhāvanā*). The fine-material and immaterial types of consciousness are involved in the practice of tranquillity meditation.

The method of tranquillity meditation

The main goal of *samatha* or tranquillity meditation is the development of concentration. Concentration or one-pointedness of mind has the characteristic of 'not being distracted'. Its function is to eliminate whatever distraction occurs, and it manifests as being unwavering or settled.

In tranquillity meditation one basic object is used, thereby excluding all other objects or experiences. The *Visuddhimagga*—a well-known Buddhist manual for the practice of meditation, written in the fifth century by the Venerable Buddhaghosa—describes in detail how forty different concentration objects can be made and used:

–   Ten material objects or *kasinas*: objects of earth (clay), water, fire or air; objects that are blue, yellow, red or white; light; and confined spaces or apertures (for example an opening in a wall)
–   Ten repulsive aspects of or stages in the decomposition of corpses.
–   Ten reflections and contemplations with regard to: the noble qualities of the Buddha, the *Dhamma* and the *Sangha*;[1] virtue, generosity, divine beings or *deva*s; our death or the various aspects of having a body; and peace
–   Four Noble Abodes: loving kindness, compassion, sympathetic joy, and equanimity

---

1. The *Sangha* is the community of people who practise the Buddha's teachings.

- Four immaterial states or domains: boundless space, boundless consciousness, nothingness, and the domain of 'neither perception nor non-perception'[2]
- The repulsive nature of food
- Concentration on the four elements of water, earth, fire and air

When practising tranquillity meditation it is important to choose an object that suits us. We need to go to a quiet place, preferably a place where there is as little distraction as possible. Then we sit down and anchor our attention in the chosen basic object. When thoughts, emotions, sounds or other experiences distract us, we note this and then return immediately to the original meditation object. This contracted and one-pointed awareness may soon give rise to a profound calmness and deep concentration. We no longer experience mental distractions and we become one with the object of meditation. We can then experience a state where we are able to visualise an object with closed eyes. Then we concentrate on this mentally visualised image until it has become well-polished, the so-called 'learning sign'.

If we are able to concentrate without interruption it is said that we have attained 'neighbourhood' or 'access' concentration (*upacāra-samādhi*). The five latent hindrances to progress in meditation—these will be discussed below—are temporarily removed. Subsequently we attain a deep state of absorption. This state is called *jhāna*; the level of concentration that is realised at this point is called absorption concentration (*appanā-samādhi*). We are then able to experience the calmness and serenity of a one-pointed mind, and the types of consciousness discussed in this chapter.

2. These four immaterial types of consciousness are discussed in chapter 6.

Fifteen fine-material types of consciousness

The fifteen fine-material types of consciousness can—just like the previous *cittas*—be divided into three groups, depicted below.

–   Five active fine-material types of consciousness

–   Five fine-material types of consciousness as the result of wholesome *kamma*

–   Five functional fine-material types of consciousness

Five active fine-material types of consciousness

Everybody knows moments of being absorbed in something. This can happen while we are engaged in sport, study or work, when making love, creating a work of art and so on. In modern psychology the term *flow* is used to describe this mental state. *Flow* is a healthy state of mind where we are so absorbed in what we are doing that we forget our small daily worries and spontaneously achieve our full potential. We temporarily do not question how or why. We do not think of success or failure but are carried along by the joy and pleasure we get from what we are doing.

The deep concentration that is developed by means of calmness meditation can be understood as a deeper form of *flow*. Because there is no physical (grosser) activity involved in the practice of tranquillity meditation, the concentration can become even stronger and subtler than when we are in *flow*. In this way we may be able to experience a state of deep concentration and realise the different levels of mental absorption, or *jhāna*. In the beginning these *jhāna*s last only for a moment, but later on they can be experienced more easily and for longer periods, depending on the circumstances and the ability of the meditator. In that sense it can be compared to a computer game: with practice we are able to achieve a more sophisticated level of the game more easily and more quickly.

The *Visuddhimagga* describes five different fine-material stages of absorption, which are developed gradually. The five fine-material types of consciousness correspond with these five *jhāna*s. They are described in the *Abhidhammattha-Sangaha* as follows:

1. The first-*jhāna* consciousness with initial application, sustained application, joy, happiness and one-pointedness
2. The second-*jhāna* consciousness with sustained application, joy, happiness and one-pointedness
3. The third-*jhāna* consciousness with joy, happiness and one-pointedness
4. The fourth-*jhāna* consciousness with happiness and one-pointedness
5. The fifth-*jhāna* consciousness with equanimity and one-pointedness

The first wholesome type of fine-material-sphere consciousness is accompanied by five mental factors, namely initial application, sustained application, joy, happiness and one-pointedness. These mental factors or concomitants of consciousness will be described in detail in part 3. In the first absorption there is already a blissful concentration, but this is still superficial because of the background noise caused by thoughts concerning the meditation instructions. These thoughts gradually disappear in the second absorption, where there are only light, subtle thoughts and sustained application. During the the third stage of concentration these subtle ripples, too, have disappeared and the meditator experiences a strong ecstatic joy. In the fourth stage this joy calms down and there is a deep state of well-being and happiness. In the last stage this feeling of happiness also dissolves into a state of concentrated absorption that is experienced as a deep ocean of serene, equanimous peacefulness.

Five fine-material types of consciousness as a result of wholesome kamma

Just as with the 'beautiful' types of consciousness discussed in chapter 4, the sublime types of consciousness can also be divided into active, resultant and functional. The five resultant fine-material types of consciousness arise by themselves as a result of previous wholesome *kamma*. They are described as follows:

1. The first-*jhāna* resultant consciousness with initial application, sustained application, joy, happiness and one-pointedness
2. The second-*jhāna* resultant consciousness with sustained application, joy, happiness and one-pointedness
3. The third-*jhāna* resultant consciousness with joy, happiness and one-pointedness
4. The fourth-*jhāna* resultant consciousness with happiness and one-pointedness
5. The fifth-*jhāna* resultant consciousness with equanimity and one-pointedness

Within the official framework of the *Abhidhamma* the sixth to the tenth type of consciousness pertain merely to rebirth. Therefore when we practise tranquillity meditation in this life we create the possibility to be reborn with one of the resultant types of consciousness that are mentioned above. The five resultant fine-material types of consciousness are not experienced by humans, but by beings in one of the sixteen fine-material spheres that will be reviewed in the next chapter.

EXCURSION: The fruits of tranquillity meditation

Abiding in *jhāna* has an extremely refreshing and calming effect. In our normal everyday lives we are often in the grip of emotions that we experience as difficult or as disturbing. In the Buddha's teachings five difficult emotions or *nīvaraṇa*s are distinguished:

– sense desire (*kāmacchanda*)
– aversion (*byāpāda*)
– dullness and sluggishness (*thīna-middha*)
– restlessness and remorse (*uddhacca-kukkucca*)
– doubt (*vicikicchā*)

It seems to be very difficult to make wise decisions when we are overwhelmed or controlled by these emotions. They often prevent us from functioning well and they repeatedly cause problems in our lives, particularly when we cannot deal with them skilfully. In a beautiful analogy our mind can be compared with water. When there is sense desire the water has lost its purity and becomes coloured; just think of how, when we are in love, we view the world through rose-tinted glasses. When there is aversion the water is brought to the boil. With dullness and sluggishness the water has become stagnant so that it loses its freshness. The water is turbulent when there is restlessness and remorse; and it is muddy or murky when there is doubt.

In the practice of *samatha* meditation the *nīvaraṇa*s become less and less prominent, and they disappear when deep concentration is achieved. The mind is clear and relaxed, temporarily free from everyday disturbances or hindrances. The effect of developing concentration and abiding in *jhāna* can be compared to taking a cool bath on a hot day. It feels good, it is cooling and refreshing, and it quickly and pleasantly relieves tiredness and tension. In daily life this can result in us being more gentle and relaxed. Furthermore, meditators who are sensitive and sufficiently motivated seem capable of developing various kinds of supernatural powers through this form of meditation. In the classical Buddhist texts the following extraordinary powers are mentioned, and we can view them literally or from a psychological perspective:

> He walks through walls or fences unhindered; he goes through mountains as if moving through air. He can enter into the ground and emerge from it. He can walk on water. Sitting cross-legged he can fly through the air like a bird. He can touch the moon and the sun. He develops a divine ear and can hear things others cannot. He can penetrate the mind of others, and develops telepathic powers. He can remember his previous lives. He develops a divine eye and can see invisible beings, as well as processes of cause and effect that are not visible with the ordinary human eye.

The Buddha and many of his disciples were said to have these powers, but the Buddha was always extremely reluctant to reveal them. He really only used them as a teaching tool to clarify a point to someone, as was the case with the Venerable Kassapa. Kassapa had developed extraordinary powers but had not yet penetrated to deeper insight. In order to show this to him the Buddha continually displayed even stronger powers than Kassapa himself, who was so impressed that he decided to become a monk, and he dedicated himself to attaining wisdom rather than achieving supernormal powers.

The Buddha did not pride himself in having these supernormal gifts and clearly stated that they were not the aim of tranquillity meditation but a by-product. They may be useful but they also have their limitations. The *jhānas* and the psychic powers that may result from them are not everlasting in nature. They are impermanent, and they require skill in dealing with them. We might be able to read every thought in the world, but if we cannot cope with desire, aggression, fear, jealousy and other emotions, these kinds of powers do not contribute at all to more harmony and inner freedom. Besides, these special powers can easily sidetrack us temporarily or permanently, and make us forget why we are walking the spiritual path. This is why the Buddha always stressed the limited merits of supernormal powers.

The practice of tranquillity meditation can provide refreshing ease and calmness, however, and in that sense it is stress reducing. Tranquillity meditation is also beneficial for people who have problems with phobias, and those who suffer concentration and sleep disorders. Clinical research has shown that people who were familiar with the practice of meditation could recover more quickly from stressful situations. And the spaciousness that arises from relaxation and peacefulness offers new creative possibilities.

Specific types of tranquillity meditation can also be extremely valuable as an antidote or remedy when we find it difficult to cope with overwhelming emotions and get stuck. Practising the Four Noble Abodes (*brahmavihāra*s) can have a softening or soothing effect when we are ruled by feelings of hatred for ourselves or others, cruelty, jealousy or too much involvement. Meditating on the different aspects of having a body may temper sensual desire, and contemplation of generosity or the *Dhamma* reinforces a basic feeling of self-confidence and security.

Tranquillity meditation can also be a good foundation for developing insight. I will say more about this in chapter 7. According to the teachings of the *Abhidhamma*, practising tranquillity meditation may result in a rebirth in one of the blissful fine-material or immaterial realms, as will be discussed in the next chapter.

....

Five functional fine-material types of consciousness

Like the functional wholesome types of consciousness reviewed in chapter 4, the last five types of consciousness in the fine-material sphere are experienced only by *arahat*s and buddhas. These types of consciousness are defined as follows:

1. The first-*jhāna* functional consciousness with initial application, sustained application, joy, happiness and one-pointedness
2. The second-*jhāna* functional consciousness with sustained application, joy, happiness and one-pointedness
3. The third-*jhāna* functional consciousness with joy, happiness and one-pointedness
4. The fourth-*jhāna* functional consciousness with happiness and one-pointedness
5. The fifth-*jhāna* functional consciousness with equanimity and one-pointedness

The next chapter describes twelve immaterial types of consciousness; together with the fifteen fine-material types of consciousness mentioned in this chapter, they are called the twenty-seven sublime or 'great realised' types of consciousness (*mahaggata-citta*s).

In *Abhidhamma* books they are often illustrated as below, and they are explained in the introduction to the next chapter.

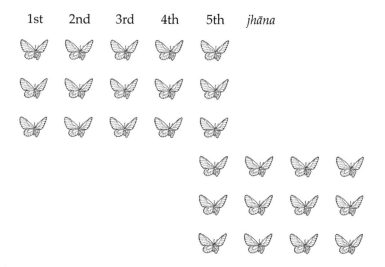

1st   2nd   3rd   4th   5th   *jhāna*

6

IMMATERIAL TYPES OF CONSCIOUSNESS

The immaterial types of consciousness can be experienced only through the practice of tranquillity meditation. The immaterial or formless types of consciousness are developed on the basis of the fifth *jhāna* (see the previous chapter). In the twelve immaterial *jhāna-citta*s can be found the same two factors of deep equanimity and one-pointedness of mind that are also present in the fifth material absorption. The immaterial types of consciousness can be subdivided into three categories:

– Four active immaterial types of consciousness

– Four immaterial types of consciousness as a result of wholesome *kamma*

– Four functional immaterial types of consciousness

Four active immaterial types of consciousness

The first four types of consciousness of the immaterial or formless sphere are related again to the practice of tranquillity meditation. The meditator first needs to get fully skilled in abiding in the *jhāna*s that were mentioned in the previous chapter. Subsequently the higher or formless *arūpa-jhāna*s can be developed. The four types of wholesome consciousness of the formless or immaterial sphere are described and explained below:

1. Wholesome *jhāna* consciousness with 'infinite space' as its object
2. Wholesome *jhāna* consciousness with 'infinite consciousness' as its object
3. Wholesome *jhāna* consciousness with 'nothingness' as its object
4. Wholesome *jhāna* consciousness with 'neither perception nor non-perception' as its object

1. When we get skilled in obtaining the fine-material *jhāna*s, and we wish to develop the formless or *arūpa-jhāna*s, we need to concentrate again on the well-polished 'learning sign' described in chapter 5. According to *jhāna* experts a vague light will appear, like the light of a firefly. When we concentrate on that light, after some time we will see nothing else but this light, which is penetrating everything and fills all space. This space is not a reality but an abstract image of reality. We concentrate on this image and think of 'infinite space' until we realise the first formless absorption consciousness. In Pali this is called *ākāsanañcāyatana-viññāṇa*.

2. Subsequently we can concentrate on the first *arūpa-jhāna* and reflect on 'infinite consciousness' until the second

formless absorption consciousness is realised in the form of
viññāṇanañcāyatana-viññāṇa.

3. In order to realise the third consciousness in the formless sphere
(*ākiñcaññāyatana-viññāṇa*) we need to take the object of the second
immaterial absorption as object and reflect on nothingness.

4. The fourth immaterial consciousness is developed by taking
the third immaterial *jhāna* consciousness as the object. In this
way we develop the fourth and highest immaterial absorption
consciousness, which in Pali is called *n'evasaññā-n'āsaññāyatana-
viññāṇa*. The English translation of this term is something like
'consciousness of the sphere where there is neither perception
nor non-perception'. I myself have never experienced these deep
stages of concentration and therefore I am fully aware of the limited explanation I am able to give here. In any case, the consciousness involved is extremely subtle.

The four immaterial *jhāna*s are mainly distinguished by the objects
of concentration. The first and the third have a concept as their
object, namely the concept of 'infinite space' and the concept of
'nothingness'. The second and the fourth absorption consciousness have the first and the third absorption consciousness as their
object.

It is not easy to develop the immaterial *jhāna*s and it requires a
long and thorough training, as well as a quiet space with little distraction. This is why these higher *jhāna*s are experienced by only a
few meditators. Therefore some readers will consider this chapter
as 'not for me'. Yet according to the *Abhidhamma* all these *jhāna*s
can be realised, as well as the four resultant immaterial types of
consciousness. In order to illustrate this I offer another excursion.

EXCURSION: Where can rebirth take place?

According to the *Abhidhamma* there are thirty-one realms or planes of existence. Some of these realms can be seen by the human eye, others are invisible.

1–4. First of all, four woeful realms are mentioned, namely:

- An invisible hell realm. We can be reborn here as the result of strong feelings of hatred. The commentaries also mention many 'sub-hells' where horrific pain and torture take place.
- The (visible) animal realm, where we will be reborn as the result of fear and ignorance.
- The realm of the 'hungry ghosts' (*petas*). Being reborn in this realm of existence is the result of obsessive (unfulfilled) desire. 'Hungry ghosts' are described as invisible beings with a very small, narrow mouth and throat, and an enormous hollow belly. These beings are always hungry and can never eat enough to fill their bellies.
- The realm of the 'jealous demigods', also called *asuras*. They are beings that were previously born as heavenly beings but who became jealous of other gods whose happiness was greater or different to theirs. As a result they fell into a lower realm, where they lead a miserable existence full of resentment and envy.

5. The fifth plane of existence is the human realm, and Buddhism considers this to be an extremely beneficial place to be born into. For human beings experience both pain and pleasure, and this means that they can easily develop wisdom. Beings in a hell realm or in the realm of the hungry ghosts experience too much pain and misery to be able to observe themselves calmly. Animals lack reflective capacity and can only act and react instinctively.

Heavenly beings or *devas* are so engrossed in their pleasurable existence that they forget to meditate and develop wisdom. That is why our existence as human beings is rated so highly; birth in the human realm, according to the Buddhist teachings, is the result of a harmonious and ethically responsible lifestyle in the past.

6–11. Six heavenly realms are then described, with each successive realm more beautiful and more enjoyable than the one before. The highest of these realms is that of the *Paranimittavasavattī-devā*, where divine beings or *devas* are the masters of, and enjoy the creations of, other divine beings. We may end up in these six heavenly realms as the result of practising generosity, loving kindness and meditation, or by performing other wholesome actions. These are realms full of happiness, sensory pleasures and peace of mind arising from the practice of concentration.

12–27. Next are sixteen planes of existence that are the domain of beings who have familiarised themselves with the fine-material levels of absorption and who are reborn with one of the five accompanying types of consciousness as wholesome result[1] in a peaceful, subtle realm. An extraordinary fine-material realm is the *Asaññasattā-bhūmi*. In this realm there are no mental processes at all; there is only a temporary fine-material form. The five *Suddhāvāsa* or 'Pure Abodes' are often mentioned in the Buddhist scriptures. They will be discussed in the next chapter.

28–31. Finally there are four immaterial levels of consciousness that can be experienced by beings that have realised the immaterial stages of absorption. They are reborn with a resultant

---

1   See chapter 5.

immaterial type of consciousness in a realm where there is no matter, but only very subtle mental processes and a high level of inner peace and happiness.

All these realms of existence are described in great detail in the Buddhist texts. They are—just like the human existence—temporary. We may remain in one realm longer than in another, but all these realms are impermanent and therefore ultimately unsatisfactory in nature.

....

The psychological interpretation of rebirth

Perhaps we find it difficult to accept this interpretation. I myself also have some reservations and unanswered questions in the area of rebirth. During meditation for example, I have had dreamlike images that I could interpret as experiences from previous lives. But these images could just as easily have arisen from a vivid imagination or from watching television. To the question about what exactly will happen after death I cannot give a definitive answer either, because I lack insight and conscious memory. In any case, I think the theory of rebirth and the transmission of *kammic* energy is quite logical and consistent. However, I cannot speak from my own experience, and I hope to get more insight into these matters when I die.

From a more pragmatic perspective there is another interpretation of the phenomenon of rebirth that can be more easily understood and accepted. In this approach, which arose later, the six realms are seen as human states of mind that can be experienced in everyday life. Sometimes we feel as if we are burning in hell, like when we are tortured in a war or burning with lovesickness. The feeling of a drug addict who cannot get his drugs in time, or the frustration we feel when we cannot get what we want, are examples of the mind state of a hungry ghost. The moment we act or react from mere instinct (through fear, hatred or the urge to survive) we live on the animal level. When we are pained by jealousy, we live like a jealous demigod. When we enjoy something and everything is going right for us, we experience a heavenly or divine state of mind. And when we practise tranquillity meditation we may taste the fine-material or immaterial realms.

In this figurative or interpersonal interpretation we experience human consciousness when we are aware of what is happening in and around us. From this type of consciousness we can make free and wise choices in life. Most of us rarely experience such moments, however. We are usually not aware and live instead on automatic pilot or conditioned by habitual patterns. Then we live on the level of animals or hungry ghosts, we experience (hellish) pain and sorrow, or we become totally absorbed in sensual pleasures, without any mindfulness.[2]

Four immaterial types of consciousness as a result of wholesome *kamma*

The *Abhidhamma* states that when we practise the four immaterial stages of concentration in this life, we have the potential to be reborn in a future life in one of the four corresponding immaterial realms. The types of consciousness with which this happens, and which in that particular life determine the nature of the *bhavaṅga*, are defined as follows:

---

2 From a Buddhist perspective human existence and human consciousness can be used well. It offers the most suitable possibility to develop liberating insight, and to break through the conditioned, ever-turning wheel of birth and rebirth. More information about this is in chapter 7.

1. Resultant *jhāna* consciousness with 'infinite space' as its object
2. Resultant *jhāna* consciousness with 'infinite consciousness' as its object
3. Resultant *jhāna* consciousness with 'nothingness' as its object
4. Resultant *jhāna* consciousness with 'neither perception nor non-perception' as its object

Four functional immaterial types of consciousness

The four functional types of consciousness of the immaterial sphere, which form the third group of immaterial types of consciousness, are experienced only by buddhas and *arahats*, and are defined as follows:

1. Functional *jhāna* consciousness with 'infinite space' as its object
2. Functional *jhāna* consciousness with 'infinite consciousness' as its object
3. Functional *jhāna* consciousness with 'nothingness' as its object
4. Functional *jhāna* consciousness with 'neither perception nor non-perception' as its object

7

SUPRAMUNDANE TYPES OF CONSCIOUSNESS

The last group of types of consciousness comprises the so-called 'supramundane' (*lokuttara*) consciousness. These types of consciousness go beyond the wheel of rebirth, or *saṃsāra*. They are the highest goal of the spiritual path, and are depicted as buddhas. According to the Buddhist teachings they can be experienced only when meditative insight is sharp enough and when the meditator and the conditions are mature. Before continuing I will first give an explanation of a second type of meditation: *vipassanā*, or insight meditation.

EXCURSION: Insight meditation

Insight meditation, called *vipassanā* in Pali, is a technique that was taught by the Buddha. It is a form of meditation that focuses on developing mindfulness so that we can learn to observe our own experiences directly and without bias or preference. We develop the ability to watch—over our own shoulder as it were—what is happening in or to us at any moment.[1]

Chapter 5 described the practice of tranquillity meditation, which has the aim of relaxation, calmness and the realisation of deep concentration. In insight meditation there will also be

---

1   Mindfulness is a wholesome mental factor; see also chapter 10.

relaxation, but it is not the main purpose of the practice. In *vipas-sanā*, relaxation is expressed in the accepting and harmonious way in which we are aware of what is most predominant in any moment: a receptive attitude to what is. Practising insight meditation is more about realising awakening and insight than realising calmness and deep concentration. While the practice of tranquillity meditation is a valuable method to de-stress tempo-rarily, the principles of insight meditation offer the potential to 'be at ease with what is'. Insight meditation gives us the tools to become aware of sources of stress, to learn to deal with these and to prevent problems and difficulties in the future that might arise through lack of awareness. We will be able to realise more hap-piness and inner freedom, and to see clearly who, what and how we are. It is a process of awakening, with the aim being to learn to deal more skilfully with the vicissitudes of life. In addition, this process of awakening leads to the development of clarity, purity of mind and intuitive wisdom.

Developing mindfulness is the main goal of *vipassanā* practice: recognising and naming or noting from moment to moment what is happening here and now. It doesn't matter what philosophy of life we have. The most important thing is to begin to study and observe our own lives in an open and honest way, without preconceptions or ideas. These observations are not made in an intellectual manner, but rather through paying close attention, and at the same time naming or noting whatever presents itself in or to us from moment to moment. We do not need to analyse, reflect on or judge what we perceive.

These accepting, non-judgemental powers of observation can be increased by meditation training. The Buddha gave guidelines that we can use when sitting, walking, lying down and standing, and also in our daily activities. In this book I will not describe these guidelines in great detail,[2] but I will offer a short description of how we can practise insight meditation when sitting or lying down.

PRACTICE: Guidelines for insight meditation when sitting or lying down

First of all it is important to adopt a posture that is easy and relaxing so that you can sit or lie down without moving for quite some time. Every time you become aware of (mentally) seeing or hearing, smelling, tasting, touching or thinking, or of a (pleasant or unpleasant) physical or mental feeling, you name or register[3] this sensation or perception without going into the content of the phenomenon. Neither do you repress, avoid or escape from the experience you observe. Whether you feel calm or tense, happy or sad, whether you feel pain or sit or lie down comfortably, it really does not matter; it is fine the way you feel in this moment.

It is particularly important to name or note as objectively as possible whatever is presenting itself, one object at a time, and always the object which at that moment is most clearly perceived. However, in order to be able to develop mindfulness more easily, it is helpful to use one object as our basic object or starting point. In this method of meditation we use the rising and falling of the abdomen. When breathing in and out the (lower) abdomen rises and falls. You will notice that the abdomen distends or rises when you breathe in, and lowers or falls when you breathe out. You can be aware of these movements.

---

2   See my first book, *Liberating Insight* (Silkworm Books, 2004).

3   Naming or labelling is a way of inner noticing that is somewhat more verbal and distinct than registering or noting. Registering or noting can be seen as a softer—less loud in volume—form of naming.

In order to get more precision in your power of observation, and to have some objective distance from what you observe, mentally naming or noting these movements is a valuable tool. The rising of the abdomen can mentally be registered as 'rising', the falling as 'falling'.

In any case you don't need to change your breathing. Breathe naturally and name the rising and falling of the abdomen as these processes occur by themselves. Naming or registering what is perceived is a tool that supports our observation, and it can be seen as a whisper in the background. While you are aware of the rising and falling of the abdomen, you name or note these movements simultaneously and accordingly.

After you have been sitting in meditation for some time, feelings of discomfort or stiffness may arise in your body. In the practice of tranquillity meditation thoughts, sounds, physical sensations or emotions are seen as distractions. In the practice of insight meditation, however, the concept of distraction or disturbance does not exist. Whatever new experience arises and presents itself, it can always be integrated as a valuable new meditation object; just as useful or valuable as the rising and falling of the abdomen. Physical feelings may become prominent; you can be aware of them and name them, as you recognise them and as long as they are predominant. You can do the same with feelings of pain, itchiness, tiredness, heaviness or lightness in the body, ease or relaxation, heat or cold. Here too, you don't need to try to get rid of the feeling or to 'observe to make them go away'. Neither do you give them extra attention. You only need to be aware of the feeling, and name or note it as it is recognised. You can do this for as long as the feeling presents itself and as long as it is perceived clearly. The same applies when you notice your mind is wandering off, you hear sounds, see images with your eyes closed or you recognise a pleasant or unpleasant emotion. Sometimes thoughts or sounds stop as soon as they are recognised. Then you don't need to do anything with them, because they have dis-appeared already. You can register the next object that presents itself. However, if the experience is still there at the moment of recognition, you can note or register as 'hearing', 'hearing', 'hear-ing'; 'thinking', 'thinking'; 'feeling', 'feeling'; 'judging', 'sadness', 'joy' and so on, as the experience presents itself and as long as it stays predominant.

It is important to point out that it is not necessary to get involved with the content of your experiences. You don't need to find out why you are thinking, why you are experiencing a certain mind state, or where, when or with whom a memory took place. On the other hand you also do not need to get rid of a thought or name it 'in order for it to go away'. It is sufficient just to observe and register thoughts, feelings and so on, as long as they are clearly there, without getting involved or trying to stop them.

So we are always observing and naming or noting whatever is happening in body and mind. Without needing to judge or anal-yse our experience, we observe and register whatever is clearly recognisable and predominant in the present moment. Noting or naming can be seen as a valuable and supportive tool, to help us be objective and to increase our powers of observation. However, the awareness of what is happening in the moment remains the most important.

When the object of observation disappears or dissolves by itself, and when at that moment nothing else is clearly recognisable, in this meditation technique you can always return to the awareness and naming or noting of the rising and falling of the abdomen as your basic object.

This, however, is just a short description of the practice of insight meditation. The bibliography in appendix 3 lists books that offer detailed descriptions of *vipassanā* meditation.

Eight supramundane types of consciousness

According to the Buddhist teachings, the practice of insight meditation leads to deep inner peace and to the realisation of a number
of carefully described stages of insight. These stages culminate in
the realisation of enlightenment, or *nibbāna*, an experience that is
described as unconditioned and supramundane. It is unrelated
to the everyday mental and physical phenomena we know, and
in Buddhism it is seen as the highest form of inner freedom and
happiness. The *Abhidhamma* explains that enlightenment is experienced by two very subtle, supramundane forms of consciousness:
magga, or path consciousness, and *phala*, or fruition consciousness.
These two types of consciousness follow one another with the
speed of lightning; the process happens so quickly that people
who experience this find it difficult to express what happened.

- Four supramundane types of path consciousness

- Four supramundane types of fruition consciousness

Four supramundane types of path consciousness

With path consciousness the everyday cognitive processes are
left behind and certain unwholesome forces, which are latently

present in us, are uprooted or extinguished.[4] According to the Buddhist texts the mind of the meditator is radically purified in that moment. This purification gradually takes place during the first four supramundane types of consciousness, and can be defined as follows:

1. *Sotāpatti* path consciousness
2. *Sakadāgāmī* path consciousness
3. *Anāgāmī* path consciousness
4. *Arahatta* path consciousness

The first moment of path consciousness completely removes three difficult tendencies, or 'fetters' (*samyojana*s).[5] These are:

- The sense of ego or self. The belief in a permanent soul or 'self', which is not based on reality, is completely eradicated. Consequently the fear of losing that with which we formerly identified disappears.
- From that moment onwards, scepticism and doubts about our potential for liberation are no longer there either. Trust in the Buddha, the *Dhamma* and the *Sangha*, and in the liberating power of meditation, has become firmly established.
- Finally superstition[6] and the belief in (and the fear of) higher powers disappear.

---

4   One of the literal translations of the term *nibbāna* is 'no longer burning'.

5   The Pali term *samyojana* literally means 'fetter or bond to existence'.

6   This refers to the belief in rites and rituals, and while these are being executed there is not really awareness of the actions nor of the underlying symbolism. Just 'mechanically' performing the rituals in question is, according to this belief, already enough to purify oneself, and it is seen as a way to control or overcome fears, or to placate a higher power. The state of mind when performing these actions is not important. All religions have some form of this type of superstition. Examples are bathing in a specific river, crossing oneself, or prostrating before an image with the idea that merely performing these actions are enough to purify the mind.

1. The first type of consciousness is called *sotāpatti-magga*, and someone who realises this is called a 'streamwinner' (*sotāpanna*).[7] A streamwinner has for the first time experienced a moment of enlightenment, and for him or her the stream of conditioned existence has been cut for the first time. It is said that a *sotāpanna* will encounter forms of desire, attachment and hatred in himself or herself, but not to such an extent that he or she will be completely overcome by them. Finally, it is said that a *sotāpanna* will, *kammic*ally speaking, only be reborn a maximum of seven times and that this rebirth will not take place in the four most woeful realms of existence described in the previous chapter. A *sotāpanna* does not necessarily have the sense that he or she is enlightened, but will naturally be inclined to realise the higher stages of enlightenment in the remaining lifetimes.

2. The second type of consciousness experiences *nibbāna* for the second time. Here the forces of sense desire and (the tendency towards) feelings of hatred, jealousy and stinginess will be strongly reduced. These driving forces are not fully extinguished but are considerably less powerful. Someone who has realised the second path consciousness is called a 'once-returner' (*sakadāgāmī*). *Sakadāgāmī*s have, *kammic*ally speaking, only a maximum of one lifetime to go before they become fully liberated from all worldly conditionings.

3. The third wholesome supramundane type of consciousness realises enlightenment for the third time. Here (the tendency towards) sense desires, hatred, stinginess and jealousy are fully extinguished. Someone who has realised this

---

7   Some authors translate the term *sotāpanna* as 'stream enterer'. This means that someone enters the stream that leads to complete liberation.

is called a 'non-returner' (*anāgāmī*). An *anāgāmī* is, according to the scriptures, no longer reborn on this earth, and has a maximum of one lifetime to live in one of the five highest fine-material realms, the *Suddhāvāsa* or 'Pure Abodes'.

4. With *arahatta* path consciousness all remaining subtle conditionings are also extinguished: forms of attachment as regards meditative absorption, pride, restlessness and all remaining blind spots. Someone who has realised the highest stage of enlightenment is called a 'fully purified one' (*arahat*). One could say that an *arahat* no longer has any mental problems and that his or her mind is as pure and clear as a mirror. Dirt from the environment can land on it but is not absorbed by it. These people no longer harm and hurt themselves or others.

I remember one time when we went on holidays to Ireland. We found an idyllic spot to camp, but suddenly we were surrounded by swarms of very small flies, midges, that were so tiny that we could hardly see them. But we felt how they bit us, as though they were vampires! The ten *samyojana*s, or fetters of existence, could be compared to these midges; they can cause trouble for ourselves and for others in various ways. When we realise *sotāpatti* path consciousness, a number of these midges disappear and we can be somewhat relieved. But there are still a lot of midges left. With the *sakadāgāmī* path consciousness a number of the remaining midges get less active, and they completely disappear with the *anāgāmī* path consciousness. With the *arahatta* path consciousness the rest of the midges disappear and we will be liberated from them once and for all.

According to the *Abhidhamma*, instead of the difficult motivating forces we normally experience and cultivate in our physical, verbal and mental activities, an enormous sense of freedom and spaciousness arises so that wholesome forces like compassion, unconditional love and wisdom can flourish. Moments when previously we were controlled by impatience, fear or lust can now be experienced and used completely differently. People who have realised this deep state of inner freedom are a light in a neurotic society.

According to the texts *arahat*s continue to live as human beings until they die, and until their death they can experience the results of previous wholesome or unwholesome deeds. They will not suffer mentally as a result, however. Because their minds have been completely purified, *arahat*s no longer act in ways that are *kammic* in nature and that create results in their consciousness. The actions of an *arahat*—as was shown in the previous chapters—are functionally wholesome (*kriyā*). When an *arahat* dies the whole process of cause and effect will end and liberation from the wheel of rebirth is complete.[8]

Four supramundane types of fruition consciousness

Immediately following and resulting from the radically purifying path consciousness, two or sometimes three moments of resultant fruition consciousness arise. This fruition consciousness is an automatic result of path consciousness, and it has *nibbāna* as its object. People who have experienced this usually describe it as an extremely blissful and peaceful experience of emptiness. The four forms of fruition consciousness correspond to the four forms of path consciousness[9] and are defined as follows:

---

8   For more information see chapter 18.

9   If one wanted it to be in sequence, a description of supramundane types of consciousness should be given in pairs: first number 1 and 5, then 2 and 6, then 3

1. *Sotāpatti* fruition consciousness
2. *Sakadāgāmī* fruition consciousness
3. *Anāgāmī* fruition consciousness
4. *Arahatta* fruition consciousness

Immediately after the succession of *magga* and *phala* the everyday or mundane processes resume. So the enlightenment experience is not permanent; it can be compared to seeing the sun for a moment on a cloudy day. According to the Buddha, and to meditators who have experienced these moments, it is extremely liberating, because in that moment forces that previously blocked and hindered us—for example desire, hatred and delusion—are completely extinguished. According to the Buddha's teachings, we can experience each of the four forms of path consciousness only once in our lifetime. The supramundane fruition types of consciousness, however, can be repeatedly experienced by skilful meditators once they have realised enlightenment. This spiritual skill is called *phala-samāpatti* and can be seen as a beneficial spiritual power.

How long does it take before we experience enlightenment?

In fact this question cannot really be answered; it depends on many factors. Some important aspects in this are motivation, dedication or commitment, the sharpness of the mind, the degree of conditioning, upbringing, health, and guidance received in the practice. In the *Mahā-Satipatthāna Sutta*, the greater discourse on the cultivation of mindfulness, the Buddha made the following statement:

---

and 7, and finally 4 and 8. In teaching these types of consciousness, preference is given to the division into active and resultant types of consciousness.

> Bhikkhus, if anyone should cultivate these four fields of mindfulness in such a way for seven years, he could expect one of two fruits: either final knowledge here and now, or, if there is a trace of clinging left, non-returning.[10] Let alone seven years—anyone who should practise them for just six years …, five years …, four years …, three years …, two years …, one year … the state of non-returner. Let alone one year—if anyone should practise them for just seven months …, six months …, five months …, four months …, three months …, two months …, one month …, or half a month … non-returning. Let alone half a month—if anyone should cultivate these four fields of mindfulness in such a way for seven days, he could expect one of two results: either final knowledge here and now, or, if there is a trace of clinging left, non-returning.[11]

In my view it will probably take quite some time for most people to experience enlightenment. However, it is good to realise that ultimately it does not matter how long we should need to practise meditation or deepen our spiritual understanding to be able to experience the happiness of *nibbāna*. For in every moment that there is mindfulness there is automatically liberating insight.[12] In this context I would like to relate the following story. A Zen student arrives at a temple and enquires: 'I would like to join your community and strive to attain liberation. How much time will I need?' The Zen master answers: 'Ten years.' The student: 'And if I work really hard, with double the effort?' The master: 'Twenty years.' The student: 'Wait a minute, that's not fair. Why did you

---

10   This refers to the level of the *anāgāmī*.
11   This is a passage from the *Dīgha Nikāya*, the Long Discourses of the Buddha.
12   See the end of chapter 17 and the beginning of chapter 18.

double the time needed?' The master: 'In your case I fear that it will take thirty years.'[13]

Forty supramundane types of consciousness

In order to be complete—and this again shows the great detail of the *Abhidhamma*—it should be mentioned that the category of supramundane consciousness is often shown to have forty instead of eight different types of consciousness:

– Twenty types of supramundane path consciousness

– Twenty types of supramundane fruition consciousness

When counting in this way it is presumed that a person has first practised tranquillity meditation and subsequently switched over to the practice of insight meditation. The five rows—from top to bottom—symbolise the five fine-material *jhāna*s, or levels of

---

13 From *After the Ecstasy the Laundry*, by Jack Kornfield.

absorption. In the row on the extreme right—from top to bottom—the immaterial *jhāna*s too can serve as a 'stepping stone to enlightenment'. In this way there are in total forty types of consciousness; in this book I will mostly use this system of forty.

So far, all one hundred and twenty-one types of consciousness mentioned in the *Abhidhamma* have been enumerated. The analysis of the human mind, however, has only been partly disclosed. In the next part of the book fifty-two mental factors or mental concomitants will be reviewed, so that we will be able to complete the puzzle of the mind.

PART THREE

MENTAL FACTORS

This part discusses the fifty-two mental factors of the various types of consciousness. Chapter 8 describes seven universal and six occasional mental factors. Chapter 9 deals with fourteen unwholesome mental factors. Chapter 10 reviews nineteen wholesome factors that arise with all wholesome types of consciousness. Chapter 11 and chapter 12 discuss the remaining wholesome mental factors, namely the three abstinences, the two illimitables, and insight or non-delusion.

8

UNIVERSAL AND OCCASIONAL
MENTAL FACTORS

Until now only a limited part of our psyche has been described. The types of consciousness reviewed in part 1 and part 2 cannot function without a number of mental factors. According to the *Abhidhamma* the one hundred and twenty-one different types of consciousness never occur by themselves. All types of consciousness need a number of mental factors, called *cetasika*s in Pali. In chapter 1 I compared this to a professional football player, but the traditional scriptures use the image of a king who is always surrounded by others. Some people look after his clothing, others whisper into his ear what he can or cannot say; some people drive him around, others protect him, and so on. Sometimes the king has a large retinue, sometimes only a handful of trusted servants, as the situation requires. But there are always some people who are accompanying him. The king can be compared to consciousness, and his helpers can be compared to the mental factors that accompany consciousness. That's why we can call them 'companions'.

The mental factors, sometimes called concomitants, always arise simultaneously with consciousness and they disappear at the same time as consciousness. They are just as short-lived as the types of consciousness mentioned in part 1 and part 2. The mental factors also have the same object and the same base[1] as the types of consciousness they correspond to.

Fifty-two mental factors

Fifty-two mental factors or *cetasika*s are enumerated. They can be divided into the following groups:

Table 8.1: Fifty-two mental factors

–   Seven universal

–   Six occasional

–   Four with ignorance

–   Three with desire

---

1   See the paragraph on the heart-base in chapter 16 for more information about bases.

- Four with aversion

- Two with dullness

- One doubt

- Nineteen universal wholesome

- Three abstinences

- Two illimitables

– One wisdom

Seven universal mental factors

The first seven mental factors, in Pali *sabbacittasādhārana-cetasika*s, play a very basic role and accompany all *citta*s. Therefore they are called 'universal', and they have been depicted as planets. These mental factors are essential to the *citta*s. They have rudimentary cognitive functions that are very difficult or (almost) impossible to distinguish separately. This can be compared to a multivitamin pill. On the jar we may read about all the different minerals and vitamins in the capsule, but we cannot taste them separately when we take the capsule. In describing the various *cetasika*s I have drawn on the work of Bhikkhu Bodhi, an American monk who wrote a valuable guide to make the *Abhidhamma* more accessible: *A Comprehensive Manual of Abhidhamma*. His descriptions of the *cetasika*s are based on old Buddhist commentaries, and they define the different mental factors by way of characteristic, function and manifestation. I find these descriptions very elucidating and have used them throughout this book. I will also use material from the *Abhidhammattha-Sangaha*, and give additional clarifications where necessary.

1. Contact or sensory impression (phassa)

The first mental factor that is mentioned is contact or sensory impression. This indicates the mental contact that arises when consciousness knows an object or 'touches' it mentally. Let's take sound as an example. Contact arises when there is a sound, the ear and ear-consciousness. If one of these three components is absent there is no contact. Therefore contact means the concurrence of consciousness, a sense faculty and a sense object. This mental factor returns in chapter 17 as one of the twelve links of dependent origination.

2. Feeling (vedanā)

Feeling is the factor that 'consumes' or experiences the object with a certain feeling tone. Here it means an elementary, affective way of experiencing an object as pleasant, unpleasant or neutral. So feeling in this sense is a lot more basic than an emotion like joy or sorrow. Let's take sense consciousness as an example: when there is seeing, hearing, smelling and tasting there is usually a neutral feeling, because it involves subtle sense organs. In the case of touch the feeling is pleasant or unpleasant, because the sense of touch is not so subtle. In this way all *citta*s are accompanied by feeling. *Vedanā* enjoys or 'tastes' the object and arises because of contact. Feeling is a penetrating and determining factor in our lives and can have a strong influence on us; therefore it is often depicted in Buddhist iconography as a man with an arrow in his eye. Feeling plays an important role in the Buddhist teachings, and it is said to be one of the five constituents of human existence (the five *khandha*s), one of the twelve links in dependent origination mentioned in chapter 17, and the second area where mindfulness can be established.[2]

---

2   More will be said about feeling in chapter 14.

3. Perception (saññā)

Perception distinguishes the qualities or details of an object. We can, for instance, in a moment of seeing consciousness distinguish a man, a woman or a particular colour. *Saññā* can also show itself as a (positive or negative) judgement of what we perceive. Finally, it plays an important part in memory. Perception has the function of making a recognisable mark or sign and so creates a frame of reference. It manifests as the interpretation of specific features of the perceived object.

In small children perception is also present, but not yet strongly developed. As we grow older and the intellect develops, perception becomes a strong factor, so that we distinguish, interpret, commit to memory and judge more and more things. Just like feeling, perception is one of the five *khandha*s.

4. Intention or volition (cetanā)

Intention too plays an important part in our lives. It has the characteristic of the wanting or the intention of a mental, verbal or physical act. Its function is to create *kamma*. It manifests as a coordinator with regard to the other mental factors. This description shows two aspects. On the one hand, intention is the initiator in performing wholesome or unwholesome *kamma* and therefore plays a very important part in the active types of consciousness. On the other hand, *cetanā* causes the other mental factors to function well while carrying out the aforementioned volitional actions. This can be compared to the care coordinator on a hospital ward. He or she has specific tasks, like facilitating a new project group. But he or she also just works along with the others on the ward and keeps an eye on things.

5. Concentration or one-pointedness (ekaggatā)

The *Abhidhamma* teaches that every type of consciousness is accompanied by concentration. Naturally the strength of the focus on what is perceived can vary greatly, but there is always concentration. The characteristic of concentration is non-wandering or non-distraction. It has the function of uniting consciousness and the object of concentration. It is manifested as peacefulness. In those moments when we feel happy or joyful, concentration can increase quickly. The Buddhist texts mention three forms of concentration:

1. Access or neighbourhood concentration (*upacāra-samādhi*). This form of one-pointedness is used in the practice of tranquillity meditation and is the basis for the realisation of the *jhānas* (see chapter 5 and chapter 6).

2. Momentary concentration (*khanika-samādhi*). This form of concentration is mainly developed in the practice of insight meditation. It is quite light and can be applied to a different object of observation at any moment.

3. Absorption concentration (*appanā-samādhi*). This form of concentration is the result of the two previous types of concentration. It can be realised when we attain the deep stages of absorption concentration or *jhāna*. In the practice of insight meditation we realise this form of concentration at the moment of enlightenment.

6. Mental vitality (jīvitindriya)

The characteristic of the sixth factor is the upkeep or maintenance of the mental factors that accompany consciousness. Just like intention works as an initiator, so vitality works as a facilitator. It manifests as the preserver of the mental factors that are present, and looks after their vitality. In that sense *jīvitindriya* may be compared to the conductor of a large choir, who keeps everyone involved and ensures that the whole choir is singing well. When someone has a burnout it can be said that the mental vitality is greatly weakened; after a holiday or after a meditation retreat we can often experience the strong presence of vitality.

7. Attention (manasikāra)

Attention is the last universal mental factor; it takes consciousness to the object. Its characteristic is to conduct the other mental factors towards the object of consciousness. Its function is to make a connection between the concomitants and consciousness; attention manifests as confrontation with an object.

Apart from this basic technical function the Buddhist teachings often mention two particular expressions of attention: *yoniso-manasikāra*, or 'wise attention', and *ayoniso-manasikāra*, or 'unwise attention'. In the first case there is wise attention or the wise judgement as to how to act or how to deal with something. In the second case there is careless, impulsive or unwise attention. Here is an example: a man we do not know starts to shout and scream at us without reason. If there is unwise attention we react impulsively with anger and we start to hit the man. If there is wise attention we don't immediately get angry, which means that there is a choice in how to deal with the situation. We may just continue on our way, for instance, without reacting to the man, or we may ask him why he is so angry. Skilful attention gives rise to wholesome types of consciousness; unskilful attention gives rise to unwholesome, woeful types of consciousness.

In order to illustrate the seven mental factors I will give a simile. When a pop musician gives a performance, the stage is lit and the amplification is switched on: this is contact, the first mental factor. The audience gets a pleasant feeling as a result: this is the second mental factor, feeling. Someone walks on stage and we recognise in this person the well-known British singer Robbie Williams; this is perception, the third mental factor. We have the intention to take everything in and to enjoy ourselves to the full: this is intention, mental factor number 4. We direct the attention to the stage (number 7) and as an immediate result we get concentrated: mental factor number 5. The degree of mental fitness that is present in us at that moment it mental factor number 6.[3]

Six occasional mental factors

The next category includes six mental factors that do not automatically arise with all forms of consciousness, and not all six are necessarily present at the same time. They can accompany wholesome as well as unwholesome types of consciousness and are called *pakiṇṇakā-cetasika*s in Pali. They are depicted as elephants (see table 8.1): not everybody rides elephants, and those who do ride elephants may have peaceful as well as less peaceful intentions.

8. Initial application (vitakka)

It is quite difficult to give a good translation of the Pali word *vitakka*. It is often translated as 'initial application'. I will try to give a description of this mental factor. *Vitakka* has the characteristic of conducting or 'elevating' consciousness to the object; its function is to strike at the object. It arises when an object is perceived and

---

3   In this example it is good to realise that the seven universal mental factors are in fact already present in every moment, but sometimes one mental factor is more predominant, at other times another, and so on.

it couples consciousness to the object, just like a train carriage is hitched or coupled to a locomotive engine. There is a subtle difference between *vitakka* and *manasikāra* (attention), the seventh mental factor that was described above. Attention is just the aiming of the mental factors to the object; *vitakka* couples the mental factors onto the object. This can be compared to a conference where an important person is going to give a speech. Together with the speaker one of the conference organisers appears on the stage from behind the wings; he makes sure that the speaker finds his way from behind the curtains and is able to present himself or herself well. This person has the task of attention. Then there is another person at the ready to introduce the speaker to the audience; this person is performing the task of *vitakka*.

Vitakka plays an important part in thinking.[4] It starts the trains of thought and accompanies the wholesome and unwholesome types of consciousness when they mentally scan an object in the function of *javana*. When *vitakka* is well-developed and maintained, it manifests as the most important factor of the first *jhāna* when consciousness is firmly coupled onto the object of concentration. In the next *jhāna*s *vitakka* is no longer present as an important factor. The speaker in the example that was given above is already known to the public and no longer needs an introduction.

When *vitakka* is present in the experience of enlightenment it is called *sammā-sankappa*, or right thought. It eliminates wrong thought and directs the mind to *nibbāna*.

9. Sustained application (vicāra)

Vicāra is often translated as 'sustained application' and is derived from the term 'wandering'. It has the characteristic of 'hovering',

---

4   Nina van Gorkom uses the term 'applied thought' as a translation of *vitakka* in her book *Abhidhamma in Daily Life*.

being on the object with continued pressure, and investigating it. Its function is the continuous application of the mental factors to the perceived object. It manifests as the anchoring of the mental factors in the object. *Vitakka* can be compared to a bee that is landing on a flower; *vicāra* is like the bee's buzzing above the flower. *Vitakka* is like striking a drum or gong; *vicāra* is like the resonance of it.

Vicāra is also translated as 'considering'. Initial application makes sure that a train of thought is started, and consideration makes sure that a thought 'continues'; it may also cause us to think the same thought over and over again. *Vicāra* too is a *jhāna* factor, and it is present in the first and second *jhāna*s. From the third *jhāna* onwards the mind quietens down so that the 'noise' of *vicāra* disappears; the mental factors no longer need to be anchored in the object of concentration.

10. Decision (adhimokkha)

The word *adhimokkha* literally means 'releasing', because decisions free the mind of doubt. The characteristic of decision is conviction; its function is non-wavering. It manifests as decisiveness, and is the opposite of doubt. Decision arises as the immediate result of something that needs to be decided on. *Adhimokkha* does not hesitate and comes to the determined conclusion of 'only this'. It can be compared to a strong pillar or to a man who is resolute and makes a decision, be it a wise decision or otherwise.

11. Effort or energy (viriya)

The term *viriya* refers to somebody who continues his or her work diligently, without break and sometimes even heroically. Energy has the characteristic of supporting, maintaining and carrying. Its function is to support the mental factors, and it manifests as not giving up. Its proximate cause is a sense of urgency, or anything that inspires vigorous action. Just as an old house is supported by new pillars, so too the mental factors are assisted and supported by energy or effort. Just as a new player can invigorate a football team, in the same way *viriya* maintains and invigorates its mental factors.

When *viriya* is applied wisely it will have many benefits, and therefore energy or effort is present in various *Abhidhamma* lists. Effort is one of the four means of accomplishment, and energy or effort in the meditative process is considered a valuable and powerful friend because it overcomes laziness and sluggishness. *Viriya* is also present in the four means of right effort, and is one of the seven factors of awakening. Finally, *viriya* is mentioned as the sixth factor in the Noble Eightfold Path in the form of 'right effort'.[5]

12. Joy (pīti)

Joy has the characteristic of endearing, or of a pleasant interest; its function is to refresh body and mind. *Pīti* gives a sense of excitement and of being deeply touched, and it manifests as elation or as rapture. Joy can be experienced with sense pleasures but also with wholesome activities, like practising generosity or meditation. According to the commentaries five grades of joy can be distinguished:

1. A light sense of joy, which may raise the hairs on the body
2. Growing, momentary joy, which can make us see flashes of light
3. Showering joy, which we experience of waves of rapture or happiness

---

5 See chapter 12 for an explanation of the Eightfold Path.

4. Uplifting joy, which makes us feel extremely light
5. Pervading joy, which pervades the whole body with feelings of happiness and rapture

Joy brings pleasure to our miserable existence and has an important place in the Buddhist teachings. A student of the Venerable Sariputta initially did not seem to make any progress in his meditation practice. Sariputta, who was known to be a very skilful meditation teacher, offered the man all kinds of practices and advice, but the man could not get to taste deeper concentration and wisdom. In despair Sariputta finally turned to the Buddha, who simply asked the man whether he enjoyed practising meditation. 'No', said the man, 'I'd rather sit in my garden daydreaming amongst the flowers.' The Buddha advised the man to just go and sit in his garden, and to note his thoughts, mental states and other experiences, without needing to judge any of them. In this way the man was able to penetrate very quickly to profound wisdom and the story had a happy ending.

Joy creates a condition for well-being. We can concentrate easily, and without too much effort we can taste the many fruits of meditation. When practising tranquillity meditation joy is one of the factors of absorption, and in insight meditation it is present as one of the seven factors of awakening.

13. Wish (chanda)

The main characteristic of *chanda* is the wish to act. Its function is searching for an object, which can be compared to stretching out a hand to pick up an object. In that sense *chanda* is much softer than the unwholesome mental factor of desire,[6] which is more greedy

---

6   See the next chapter.

and attaches itself to the object. *Chanda* manifests as the wish and the intention to experience an object; this object is at the same time the proximate cause for *chanda*. In the Buddha's teachings three kinds of *chanda* are distinguished:

1. Sense desire (*kāmacchanda*). Ethically speaking this form of *chanda* is unwholesome, because sense desire easily leads to suffering and delays the realisation of ultimate happiness. Therefore *kāmacchanda* is mentioned as one of the five hindrances to spiritual growth.

2. The wish to do (*kattukamyatā-chanda*). This is the functional wish to stretch out an arm, for instance, or to go to the bathroom. This form of *chanda* is of no ethical (wholesome or unwholesome) value.

3. The desire or wish for deeper wisdom (*Dhammacchanda*). This wholesome wish can move us to devote ourselves to the practice of meditation and to search for deeper wisdom.

The six occasional mental factors together with the seven universal mental factors are called *aññasamāna*, or 'in collaboration with both'. They can work together with both wholesome and unwholesome types of consciousness. We may strive for a noble cause, or for harmful goals. We may rejoice in an act of loving kindness, or we may try to cheat someone. The next chapter mentions fourteen mental factors that are linked only to unwholesome types of consciousness.

9

UNWHOLESOME MENTAL FACTORS

This chapter will discuss unwholesome mental factors. These factors increase our suffering and can easily block the realisation of deeper happiness and wisdom. They collaborate with the twelve unwholesome types of consciousness mentioned in chapter 2. The fourteen unwholesome or *akusala cetasika*s are:

– Four with ignorance as their leader

– Three with desire as their leader

– Four with hatred as their leader

– Two with dullness as their leader

– One doubt

Four with ignorance as their leader

The first four unwholesome concomitants are present in all types of unwholesome consciousness. They have ignorance as their 'leader', because this mental factor plays a prominent role in all four of them. A description of these factors is given below.

14. *Ignorance or delusion (moha)*

Ignorance itself has mental blindness or unknowing as its characteristic. Its function is 'not penetrating to the reality of what is happening at the present moment', and concealing or veiling reality. It manifests as mental darkness or as the absence of insight. Its proximate cause is unwise attention, *ayoniso manasikāra* (see mental factor number 7 in the previous chapter). Ignorance has nothing to do with intelligence; even the most erudite people can act out of confusion and a lack of 'life intelligence'. Ignorance is depicted as a pig. Just as a pig prefers to wallow in mud, in the same way we have problems time and time again because of ignorance.

Sometimes ignorance has the nature of not clearly understanding what is happening in the moment; this is called *āpatti-patti-avijjā*. Examples of this are thoughtlessness and not, or not in time, being aware of inner signals, as can be the case with health problems. We may plod on for a long time until eventually we have so many problems that we have to call in sick at work or go and see the doctor. And sometimes it may even be too late to recover completely.

A second and much stronger form of ignorance is called *micchāpattipatti-avijjā* in Pali. In this case we ignore the reality of the moment, and we are greatly deluded. With this type of ignorance we may realise that we are overworked, but we ignore this signal, even though we know better. This type of ignorance can be very harmful and can easily lead to forms of addiction. We know quite well that it is bad for our health to smoke a lot or to drink alcohol, but we do it anyway.

In fact we all know these two types of ignorance, whether we like it or not. They play an important role in deeply rooted human patterns. When I look at myself I notice that for a large part of the day I am unaware, not knowing what is really happening in the moment. And I often catch myself taking another cup of coffee even though I have intestinal problems and I know that drinking coffee will only make them worse.

15. Shamelessness or lack of embarrassment (ahirika)

The characteristic of shamelessness is the absence of disgust or embarrassment as regards unwholesome or inappropriate behaviour. Shamelessness is expressed as not hesitating to show behaviour that causes pain and suffering. It arises from lack of self-respect; we no longer make an effort to look at ourselves with respect.

16. Lack of scruples or fearlessness of wrongdoing (anottappa)

Lack of scruples, or ethical carelessness, is characterised by the absence of fear and respect for the consequences of ethically unwholesome behaviour. The function, manifestation and proximate cause are the same as those of shamelessness. *Ahirika* and *anottappa* can be seen as two cousins affecting our conscience. Shamelessness is concerned with how we look at ourselves, and is described in the *Abhidhamma* as not being embarrassed to pick up a ball of manure. Lack of scruples is related to how others look at us, and is compared to picking up a hot iron ball. Because the difference between a hot and a dirty ball is difficult to depict, the illustrator has depicted *ahirika* as a big dog poo with flies around it, and *anottappa* as a red-hot kettle. The wholesome opposites of *ahirika* and *anottappa* will be described in the next chapter.

17. Restlessness (uddhacca)

Restlessness or agitation has the characteristic of turmoil, and can be compared to water that is being stirred up by the wind. Its function is to destabilise, and it manifests as being stirred up and agitated. Its proximate cause is careless attention. Because restlessness can sometimes be extremely dominant it gets mentioned as the twelfth unwholesome type of consciousness.[1]

The first four unwholesome mental factors arise with all unwholesome types of consciousness. Sometimes one factor is predominant, sometimes another. I remember, for instance, how as a teenager I now and again took part in petty thefts from shops. At times I felt only confused (*moha*). At other times I said to myself that I didn't do anything wrong and couldn't care less that I had stolen from a small shop, because I knew that the owner could just about keep going financially (*ahirika*). Sometimes I was undeterred by fear of criticism from my parents (*anottappa*). Finally, I often felt restless during the thefts (*uddhacca*) but yet could not

---

1   See chapter 6.

refrain from stealing. So the power or intensity of these *cetasikas* varies, but all four of them are present.[2]

Three with desire as their leader

The next three unwholesome mental factors—and all three are clearly related to desire, and therefore are depicted as a cock—are mainly connected to the first eight unwholesome types of consciousness described in chapter 2.

18. Desire or attachment (lobha)

I have already discussed desire, in chapter 2. I would like to add here that *lobha* includes selfish desire as well as hankering and attachment. Whereas *chanda* (the thirteenth mental factor) can be expressed in wholesome as well as unwholesome ways, desire is only manifested in an unwholesome manner. If desire is not dealt with skilfully, it increases suffering or (temporarily) blocks the experience of deeper happiness. Desire has the characteristic of grasping an object. Its function is to stick to the object, just like a fly sticks to a fly strip. *Lobha* manifests as perseverance, just like a pitbull terrier does not want to let go of its prey. Its proximate cause is seeing pleasure or happiness in things that in reality only lead to addiction or dependence. Desire is viewed as the direct cause of our suffering, whereas ignorance is seen as the indirect or less visible cause.

In the Buddhist scriptures desire is often compared to the behaviour of a cock, for two reasons. One is that a cock never has

---

2   Fortunately I was caught in the act after a while, and this gave me such a fright that I immediately stopped stealing. The opposites of the first four unwholesome *cetasikas* were victorious.

enough to eat. And the second is that a cock spends a lot of time chasing the hens, and in that sense also 'never gets enough of it'.

19. Wrong view (diṭṭhi)

Diṭṭhi means seeing or view, but it is mostly used in the sense of 'wrong view' (micchā-diṭṭhi). Its characteristic is an incorrect or coloured interpretation of reality as it shows itself. Its function is to have presumptions. Wrong view manifests as an incorrect interpretation or as a delusion. Its proximate cause is unwillingness to see reality as it is. Buddhist psychology enumerates sixty-two forms of wrong view. In summary it can be said that we cherish diṭṭhi when we interpret things or experiences as satisfactory or as permanent, whereas in fact they cannot give everlasting happiness and are impermanent. Or we interpret things as belonging to us, whereas in reality we are not the owner (of people, of a position, of thoughts, emotions, and so on). Finally diṭṭhi is also present when we judge behaviour that is ethically doubtful as being positive, which leads to delusion.

20. Pride (māna)

Pride or conceit has the characteristic of feeling superior to others, or on the other hand of feeling inferior to others. It easily arises when we compare ourselves to others. Māna paves the way for self-glorification and manifests as vanity. The Buddhist teachings see conceit or pride as a delusion or fallacy that arises from desire.

Wrong view and conceit are two different expressions of desire. Both are always accompanied by desire, but conceit never occurs simultaneously with wrong view. The reason is that the object is different in nature. Wrong view concerns ideas we are attached to, while conceit is mainly aimed at comparing ourselves with others.

Desire, wrong view and conceit are also called the three *papañcas*, or proliferations, because these three mental factors can be quite strong and may cause us to engage in all kinds of extreme behaviour.

Four with hatred as their leader

The next four mental factors (depicted as snakes) are associated with the types of consciousness that are rooted in hatred or aversion.

21. Hatred or aversion (dosa)

Hatred is known for its destructive force, and it can express itself as rage, enmity, resentment, irritation, sadness, fear or resistance. Hatred is wild and cruel in nature, and spreads like snake poison that permeates our whole body. *Dosa* manifests as the tendency to reproach and accuse. Hatred usually arises due to unwise attention as regards unpleasant feelings. The Buddha compared hatred with a snake. If we don't see or recognise a snake, we may easily step on it and get bitten. Hatred can act on its own, but it can also be accompanied by one of the following three mental factors.

22. Envy (issā)

The characteristic of envy is being jealous of others' success. Envy manifests as dissatisfaction and aversion, and arises when we see the success and good fortune of others.

23. *Stinginess (macchariya)*

Stinginess or meanness always has to do with concealing our own success or wealth, and with the unwillingness to share our good fortune. This factor manifests as shrinking away from sharing when the occasion is there, and as a sour feeling. It is the opposite of generosity. Stinginess arises as the result of our own success, happiness, fame or good fortune.

24. *Feelings of guilt or remorse (kukkucca)*

Remorse has feeling regret as its characteristic and it makes us sad. It arises as a reaction to mistakes we made or unwholesome actions we performed. Remorse may also arise as a reaction to having omitted to do wholesome acts. In Buddhism *kukkucca* is seen as an unwholesome factor, because there is clearly an aversion as regards our actions. This is contrary to puritanical or Calvinistic cultural conditioning, which appears to view feelings of guilt or regret as a virtue. The *Abhidhamma* states that *kukkucca* may indirectly lead to an increased ethical sensibility, because remorse invites us to improve our conduct.

Two with dullness as their leader

The next two concomitants are concerned with a mind that, according to Buddhist psychology, is 'discouraged from the object'. They are depicted as dozing cats.

25. Dullness of the mind (thīna)

Dullness or sluggishness of the mind has the characteristic of lack of driving power, and it dispels the remaining energy. It manifests as the sinking of the mind.

26. Torpor of the mental factors (middha)

Here there is a subtle technical difference: while mental factor number 25 works on consciousness, number 26 is more concerned with sluggishness and inertia of the mental factors. However, I must confess that in practice I find it difficult to make this distinction. I suspect that my state of mind is not clear enough when there is dullness to confirm this detailed analysis of the *Abhidhamma*.

Middha has the characteristic of stiffness or unwieldiness, and functions as stifling and smothering. It manifests as lethargy, nodding off and sleepiness. Both mental factors arise because of unwise attention to sleepiness and boredom, and they can be seen as a sickness. They belong to the list of unwholesome factors, for dullness temporarily incapacitates us in making wise decisions and reacting appropriately to stimuli.

Doubt

27. Doubt (vicikicchā)

This last unwholesome factor does not refer to doubts we may have about things like whether we will have a cup of tea or a cup of coffee. Doubt rather refers to the absence of a deeper or spiritual confidence. In the Buddhist teachings doubt means a lack of confidence in the Buddha, the *Dhamma* and the *Sangha*, and in the path leading to liberating insight. Doubt destabilises us and makes us falter and waver. Therefore in the drawing doubt is depicted as weighing scales. It manifests as indecisiveness and as being thrown to and fro between one point of view and another. Doubt arises because of unwise attention and has different aspects. It may manifest, for example, as mistrust, disbelief or as lacking in self-confidence.

Many unwholesome mental factors arise as a result of unwise attention. This offers opportunities for a way of living where we need not be so controlled by the unwholesome mental factors. For when we develop mindfulness (the second wholesome mental factor discussed the next chapter) we are in a much better position to prevent the arising or proliferation of the unwholesome mental factors. This is why I would see the teachings of the *Abhidhamma* as 'mirroring'. On the one hand it offers us a mirror so that we can see the workings of our mind. On the other hand it offers the potential for a happier life, because when we cultivate mindfulness we will no longer be so much at the mercy of the unwholesome mental factors mentioned in this chapter.

10

WHOLESOME MENTAL FACTORS

This chapter discusses the nineteen universal wholesome mental factors, or *sobhana-sādhārana-cetasika*s. These factors decrease our suffering, and increase profound happiness as well as inner and social harmony. These 'universal beautiful' concomitants or mental states are depicted as flowers, and they are present in all wholesome moments of consciousness, namely the twenty-four wholesome, the twenty-seven sublime and the forty supramundane types of consciousness.

– Nineteen universal wholesome mental factors

28. Confidence or faith (saddhā)

According to the *Visuddhimagga*, the characteristic of *saddhā* is placing trust in something or someone, or the presence of faith and confidence. The function of confidence is to purify, like a detoxing homeopathic medicine, and it helps us to face difficulties. It manifests as clarity and as decisiveness, or as a resolute attitude. The proximate cause for the arising of confidence is called

saddheyya-vatthu in Pali: an object that calls forth inspiration or
confidence. Examples of this are:
–   Seeing or listening to somebody who radiates peacefulness
    and wisdom.
–   The realisation that we do or have done something benefi-
    cial for our own well-being or for the well-being of others,
    or both.
–   To maintain spiritual friendships; in Buddhism this is con-
    sidered something extremely wholesome.
–   To experience the benefits of meditation.
–   To reflect on our ability to deal wisely with difficult situa-
    tions in life, like illness, pain, fear and sadness.

Confidence or faith is the foundation of performing wholesome
deeds like generosity, of ethically appropriate behaviour and
of patience. This trust in 'that which is good', also called *pakati-
saddhā*, is extremely valuable and causes us to take up, for instance,
the practice of meditation. However, it is still faith that is somewhat blind. For we do not yet have any real meditation experience,
and we mainly go by what others have told us about the beneficial effects of meditation. Or we are inspired by something we
have read, without having experienced it for ourselves.

Through our own direct meditation experience a second form
of faith or confidence arises: *bhāvanā-saddhā*. This confidence is
based on our own experience of the fruits of meditation, and goes
much deeper than just trusting in 'that which is good'. Confidence
or trust is the opposite of sceptical doubt, and it is mentioned as
one of the five healing powers (*balas*).[1]

---

1   See appendix 1.

29. Mindfulness (sati)

The Pali word *sati* is used in reference to remembering something. Usually remembering is connected with something from the past; mindfulness, however, it points to the present and it can also be defined as 'to remember what is happening in and to us *in the present moment'*. Mindfulness has two aspects. On the one hand there is an open and allowing awareness of what is happening in or to us in the present moment as a physical, mental, sensory or emotional experience. On the other hand there is a subtle, non-identifying noting of what is presenting itself: the mental naming or registering of the experience that is perceived in the moment.

The characteristic of mindfulness is an unwavering presence of mind. Its function is not to forget, ignore or skip over what is predominant in the moment. Mindfulness manifests as being face to face with what is happening in the moment in body or mind. It expresses itself as a 'guardian angel' against being unconsciously (further) conditioned by thoughts, emotions and sense stimuli.

Mindfulness offers a tool to deal skilfully with difficulties, and it can prevent unwholesome mind states and unnecessary mistakes. It is supported by a balanced effort and is caused by a keen perception. Mindfulness or bare attention offers us the potential to develop liberating insight.[2]

The *Satipaṭṭhāna Sutta*, a well-known discourse by the Buddha, mentions four areas (*satipaṭṭānas*) where mindfulness can be developed, namely the body,[3] feelings or *vedanā*,[4] consciousness and the remaining mental factors. Cultivating mindfulness in these four fields is the foundation for the practice of *vipassanā*

---

2 See chapter 12 for the various aspects of insight.
3 See part 4.
4 *Cetasika* number 2; see chapter 8.

or insight meditation, as was discussed in chapter 7. The Buddha concluded the *Satipaṭṭhāna Sutta* with the words: 'Monks, this is the direct path for the purification of beings, for the overcoming of sorrow and lamentation, for the disappearance of pain and discontent, for acquiring the true method, for the realisation of *nibbāna*, namely, the four *satipaṭṭhāna*s.'

30. Moral shame (hiri)

The characteristic of moral shame or embarrassment is the disgust as regards behaviour that is causing harm or pain. It works as a preventative against ethical lapses. Embarrassment manifests as refraining from shameful behaviour.

31. Fear of wrongdoing (ottappa)

The characteristic of *ottappa* is wholesome fear of committing harmful or painful acts. The function and manifestation are the same as those of moral shame. Moral shame and fear of wrong-doing are often mentioned as a pair, and they constitute the ingredients of our conscience. Shame is internal, whereas moral carefulness or fear of wrongdoing is more concerned with the external world. They are also called the two *lokapala*: protectors of the world. For when *hiri* and *ottappa* are well developed, happiness and harmony will increase in the world. Moral shame and fear of wrongdoing are the opposites of shamelessness and lack of scruples, mental factors number 15 and 16 that were reviewed in the previous chapter.

32. Non-greed (alobha)

Alobha is the opposite of desire or greed, mental factor number 18 that was mentioned in the previous chapter. Non-greed has the characteristic of lack of desire, or not clinging to an object, just as raindrops on a windowpane are not sucked in through the glass but just drip down. Its function is not laying claims to something, and it manifests as a non-attached attitude. *Alobha* is expressed in passive and active forms. The passive expression, which refers to the literal translation of the Pali as non-desire, can be seen as an unobtrusive participant, namely as not being attached to an object. When we develop mindfulness, for example, *lobha* shows itself as a non-attached, non-identifying awareness of what is presenting itself. It is present, but not so noticeable, whereas mindfulness and the experience that is perceived play a much more conspicuous role. As an active manifestation *alobha* plays the main part, and shows itself as unselfishness or as generosity (*dāna*), for example when we offer somebody our support or give them a present. Both roles are seen as extremely wholesome. *Alobha* is like a cool breeze on a hot day, or like an oasis in a world where we usually (unconsciously) pour oil on the fires of desire and attachment.

33. Non-hatred or benevolence (adosa)

The characteristic of non-hatred is not being vindictive; it refers to the absence of resentment and cruelty. Non-hatred puts all irritation aside and manifests as well-being. *Adosa* too has a passive and an active aspect. The passive expression, namely as non-hatred, is again an inconspicuous but beneficial participant. In the practice of insight meditation it is present in this way as the mild and accepting attitude towards the experiences that present themselves. When we feel explicitly friendly, and during the practice of loving kindness meditation, the active side of *adosa* plays the main part and manifests as benevolence. In Buddhist philosophy this aspect of *adosa* is often called *mettā*, or loving kindness. I will say more about *mettā* in the next chapter, when introducing the Four Noble Abodes.

34. Equanimity (tatramajjhattatā)

Equanimity (literally, 'being there in the middle') refers to an inner equilibrium and impartiality. The characteristic of this wholesome mind state is to balance the relationship between consciousness and the *cetasika*s. Its function is to prevent extremes (deficiency or excess), while equanimity manifests as neutrality. It is compared to a judge who listens objectively to all parties without preference. In Pali equanimity is also called *upekkhā*. In the Buddha's discourses it is mentioned as one of the seven factors of awakening, and as one of the Four Noble Abodes.

35, 36. Serenity of the mental factors and of consciousness (passaddhi)

The last twelve universal wholesome mental factors can be arranged in pairs. These mental factors have a wholesome effect on consciousness or on the mental factors. Particularly in the meditation process these pairs are developed more and more; but to be honest, in real terms I find it difficult to distinguish between them.

Serenity has the characteristic of calming disturbances. It manifests as peacefulness and as coolness. It is the opposite of stress, unrest and worry.

37, 38. Lightness of the mental factors and of consciousness (lahutā)

Lightness removes heaviness and is the opposite of dullness and lethargy. It manifests as non-sluggishness and being flexible in nature.

39, 40. Malleability of the mental factors and of consciousness (mudutā)

Malleability or flexibility reduces mental rigidity. It manifests as non-resistance, and it is the opposite of unwholesome mental states such as conceit and wrong views.

41, 42. Wieldiness of the mental factors and of consciousness (kammaññatā)

Wieldiness, sometimes translated as adaptability or workability, removes unwieldiness of consciousness and its concomitants. It manifests as easy and successful functioning of the mind. It is the opposite of desire, anger and other mental states that reduce the flexibility of the mind, such as dullness and stinginess.

43, 44. Proficiency of the mental factors and of consciousness (pāguññatā)

The characteristic of this mental factor is the sense of having a strong or healthy mind: we feel strong and fit, and we are able to cope with sources of stress. Its function is to increase health, and proficiency is manifested as the absence of disability. It is the opposite of doubt.

45, 46. Rectitude of the mental factors and of consciousness (ujjukatā)

Rectitude means straightforwardness and honesty; its function is to stop tortuous and deluding mental states. It manifests as non-crookedness, and it is the opposite of hypocrisy, fraudulence, mendacity and so on.

The abovementioned nineteen 'beautiful' mental states are always present in every wholesome moment of consciousness, either as dominant forces or as almost invisible players in the background. However, they always arise and pass away simultaneously with every wholesome type of consciousness.

11

ABSTINENCES AND ILLIMITABLES

The last six of the fifty-two *cetasikas* are occasionals that do not arise automatically when we perform a wholesome deed. They are guests who bring happiness, and they come and go when the right conditions are present. This chapter describes the three so-called abstinences and the two illimitables. The next chapter discusses the last mental factor, wisdom or insight.

– Three abstinences:

– Two illimitables:

Three abstinences (*virati*)

47. *Right speech (sammā-vācā)*
48. *Right action (sammā-kammanta)*
49. *Right livelihood (sammā-ājīva)*

The three abstinences, or *virati*, have to do with deliberately refraining from or no longer engaging in unwholesome behaviour as regards speech, actions or livelihood. Right speech—depicted as a tongue—means that we do not intentionally tell lies, gossip, use inappropriate language and talk nonsense. Right action—depicted as a gun—refers to refraining from killing, stealing, acting sexually in ways that are harmful[1] and (excessive) use of alcohol and drugs. Right livelihood, the third abstinence, concerns not or no longer having a profession or hobby, or no longer engaging in activities where we harm ourselves and others; examples of this are making a living as a burglar (see drawing) or by selling drugs, or hunting just for pleasure.

To illustrate: Trudy can be mean when gossiping with a colleague. Suddenly she realises that what she is doing is ethically unsound, and that by acting in this way she will not make anyone happy. She then consciously stops gossiping. At that moment right speech is present. The same abstaining principle applies with right action and with right livelihood. The Buddhist texts mention three levels of renouncing or abstaining:

1. Natural renunciation. This means deliberately preventing or stopping harmful, destructive behaviour. Depending on our lifestyle, upbringing and social position, this ethical antenna appears when unwholesome behaviour could arise or has already arisen, and it protects us from (more) unnecessary suffering.

2. Renunciation by choosing to follow ethical guidelines or precepts. Many Buddhists participate in a short ceremony to take five ethical precepts as guidelines for the way they live their lives. They undertake not to kill, not to steal, not to have harmful sexual conduct, not to tell lies and not to take

---

1   This means sexual contact with the use of violence, or when there is inequality of power.

alcohol and drugs (to such an extent that the ability to make ethical distinctions gets undermined).

3. Renunciation by uprooting. This form of renunciation is definite, and takes place with the enlightenment experience, with the supramundane path consciousness.

The three abstinences have the characteristic of not transgressing ethical boundaries through unwholesome speech, actions and livelihood. They cause us to refrain from behaviour that could hurt or harm. They manifest as the absence of unwholesome conduct. They arise as the direct result of other wholesome qualities, like confidence, shame and wisdom. They can be compared to the revulsion a wise king feels to making mistakes. The three abstinences play an important role as the ethical factors of the Eightfold Path. They ensure that we begin to show behaviour that is less destructive. In that sense they are the foundation for a virtuous and harmonious life *and* for walking the spiritual path to wisdom.

Two illimitables (*appamaññā*)

The term 'illimitables' refers to the universal character of these two factors; therefore they are depicted as the symbols for eternity or infinity. They can be developed and 'radiated' in the broadest sense to all living beings, without exception.

50. Compassion (karunā)

Compassion is the fiftieth mental factor of consciousness. The characteristic of compassion is the wish to diminish or remove suffering. Compassion is the direct opposite of cruelty or malice; it manifests as the absence of cruelty. In society it leads to greater empathy, social responsibility or commitment, and to selfless service. When we develop compassion we should not mistake pity for compassion. This confusion may arise when we are overwhelmed by sorrow. In that sense compassion is a warm but at the same time non-attached mercy. Developing compassion is of enormous benefit in coping with pain and adversity in ourselves, and also when we are confronted with the suffering of others.

51. Sympathetic joy (muditā)

Sympathetic joy can be considered the wholesome opposite of envy and jealousy. Often we may be consumed by envy, but this tendency can be toned down by developing *muditā*, and it can be transformed into feelings of sympathetic joy. Sympathetic joy is not only a feeling of joy or cheerfulness; it shows itself as being joyfully sympathetic with the material or immaterial good fortunes of others. *Muditā* is congratulatory in nature and causes resistance to melt away.

EXCURSION: The Four Noble Abodes

In Buddhism, compassion and sympathetic joy are seen as two of the Four Noble Abodes, or *brahmavihāras*. This refers to four 'good friends' or forms of 'divine abiding' that contribute to greater harmony in society: loving kindness, compassion, sympathetic joy and equanimity. These four wholesome mind states can be developed towards ourselves and towards others. They have great healing power and may contribute to increased inner and social happiness. I would like to discuss the other two *brahmavihāras* or noble qualities below.

Loving kindness (*mettā*)

Loving kindness, or unconditional love, is the active aspect of non-hatred, *cetasika* number 33 (see previous chapter), and as such it is called *mettā* in Pali. The characteristic of *mettā* is promoting the welfare of ourselves and others. Its function is to put irritation aside, and to be concerned for or involved in the welfare of ourselves and others. Loving kindness manifests as a warm, helpful attitude, and as loveliness.

'In this world hatred is never ceased by hatred; it is only truly ceased by love. This is an eternal law', says the fifth verse of the *Dhammapada*, a well-known Buddhist text of aphorisms. *Mettā* refers to gentleness and friendliness. It is open, unbounded or unlimited, and does not expect anything in return. *Mettā* is the opposite of hatred.

If not practised correctly loving kindness meditation practice may easily lead to attachment or sentimentality. The proximate cause for the arising of *mettā* is seeing the goodness in ourselves and in others.

PRACTICE: Loving kindness meditation
••

Sit in a comfortable manner, close your eyes and see if you can wish something wholesome for yourself, for example the wish: 'May I be happy, free from pain, danger, hunger and thirst.' Or 'May I be free from sorrow, fear, and other forms of pain or frustration.' You can use these words or—if you prefer—choose phrases that come up in the moment, and repeat these in a calm, relaxed way. If resistance or distracting thoughts come up, note these, but at the same time continue the exercise.

After some minutes you do the same for somebody you respect or love very much. Someone we might call a benefactor.[2] Next you send kind thoughts to your friends, relatives and colleagues, then to the people you only know superficially (the shopkeeper, the neighbours and so on), and then to all the people in your town or village. Then you extend the circle and let your thoughts of kindness radiate to all the people in your county or state, then to your fellow countrymen, to all those who live in the same continent as you, and finally to all the people in the whole world.

You can also incorporate animals into the practice, and if you believe in them you can also send thoughts of loving kindness to invisible beings in blissful or miserable realms or mental states. Finally you can conclude the practice with a comprehensive wish like: 'May I and all other living beings be happy, free from pain, resentment and danger. May all living beings be free from suffering and live in peace and harmony.' Remain seated quietly for a minute or so, and slowly return to the present.

Loving kindness meditation always starts with ourselves, because it is said that we cannot truly have unconditional love if we cannot have *mettā* for ourselves. From this basis *mettā* is radiated in ever-increasing circles to our surroundings. Finally the whole universe is bathed in loving kindness and goodwill. In the texts eleven benefits of *mettā* are mentioned:

1. We can sleep well.
2. We wake up peacefully.

---

2   When you are practising loving kindness meditation for longer periods of time, it is suggested not to send *mettā* to your loved one or to a person you have sexual feelings about. This prevents *mettā* from turning into a passionate state of mind.

3. We have pleasant dreams.
4. We are automatically loved by ourselves and by others.
5. We are loved by beings in invisible realms of existence, and by animals.
6. We are protected by heavenly beings or *devas*.
7. We are protected against dangers like poison, weapons, fire, fear or aggression.
8. Our face becomes radiant.
9. Our mind becomes peaceful.
10. We live and die without confusion.
11. We will be reborn in blissful realms.

When we apply this traditional list of benefits to our Western society, we can see that developing loving kindness has the following wholesome effects:

- Loving kindness leads to greater relaxation; we are able to deal better with stress, and we will recover more quickly from stress-related complaints.
- It results in better social skills and in higher emotional intelligence.
- Developing loving kindness results in a stronger sense of basic security and self-acceptance. Particularly in Western society, where many people suffer from low self-esteem, *mettā* can have a valuable healing influence on this 'disease'.
- We gain peace of mind, and thereby greater creativity.
- We are less ruled by feelings of hatred and fear.
- Loving kindness can function as a solid foundation for the practice of insight meditation.

Equanimity (upekkhā)

Equanimity, the last of the Four Noble Abodes, can be seen as a stabilising force. It gives us the capacity to see with wisdom people and situations in the right proportions, and not to be blinded by attachment or aversion. As a concomitant it can be found as the thirty-fourth mental factor.

Equanimity has the characteristic of impartiality. It looks at the loved and the unloved, the pleasant and the painful, the fortunate and the unfortunate, the wholesome and the unwholesome in living beings and circumstances from an equanimous point of view. *Upekkhā* is the remedy for (extreme) passion and feelings of hatred. However, it should not be confused with indifference, which is unconscious and dull in character. While loving kindness, compassion and sympathetic joy clearly have an aspect of being involved and connected, with equanimity this is transcended. This can be a great relief, particularly in situations where we cannot or do not want to take action. Sometimes we cannot change other people's unwholesome behaviour, but we might not be able to view it with kindness or compassion either. In those cases it can be liberating to realise that others will experience the result of their actions the most. Reflecting like this can offer a sense of balance and proportion.

To understand the function of the Four Noble Abodes in Buddhist psychology, we can use the analogy of a mother with four children. Her wish for a good education and upbringing for her youngest child can be compared with the good wish of loving kindness. Her second child is ill, and her wish for the child to get better is the manifestation of compassion. At present all is going well for her third child; her sympathetic joy and her wish for the continuation of his well-being is *muditā*. The oldest child is independent and can look after himself. She knows he is going his own way, and she does not need to concern herself with him; in this there is equanimity.

These four mental states can be developed as specific meditations, and they promote harmony in ourselves and in society. Besides being developed through formal meditation, the four *brahmavihāras* can also be cultivated quite simply in daily life. Some examples:

- When saying goodbye, or when meeting or passing somebody in the street, mentally make the wish that he or she may be happy.
- Before or after a meal, mentally give thanks to the people who provided your food.
- Do social work or be of service; help friends or relatives.
- Support a good cause.
- Pay colleagues or friends a compliment from time to time.
- Do not hesitate to congratulate people on their success or good fortune.
- When you have a certain aversion to somebody's behaviour, reflect on the fact that he or she will ultimately suffer most, and that they will bear the consequences of their unwholesome behaviour.
- When you are inclined to take on too many responsibilities, reflect from time to time that you are not responsible for all the mistakes and breakdowns in communication in an organisation.
- If you are quite a perfectionist and are sometimes suffering because of this, then reflect that imperfection is part of life, that we cannot always get nine or ten out of ten, and that seven out of ten is often good enough.

A good book with clear explanations and practical meditation exercises concerning the *brahmavihāra*s is *Lovingkindness* by Sharon Salzberg, an American meditation teacher.

Developing and integrating the four *brahmavihāra*s gives satisfaction and a deeper meaning to our lives. It is a skilful way to transform troublesome or persistent tendencies into wholesome forces. In this way we experience greater harmony and make the world a more beautiful and more joyful place.

12

WISDOM

Wisdom or insight (*paññā* in Pali) is depicted as an owl, and it is the last mental factor (number 52). Wisdom investigates and penetrates the truth of things. It brings light to the darkness, creates clarity, and is the opposite of misunderstanding, delusion or ignorance (*avijjā*). Wisdom or insight is not just the intellectual capacity to consider things in relation to other things; it refers specifically to a deep intuitive understanding of reality as it appears in the present moment, without using 'step by step' reasoning. It is the fruit of concentrated awareness or mindfulness and goes a lot deeper than thought.[1] In the Pali literature various synonyms are given for wisdom. The most prevalent ones are *vipassanā* (insight), *dhamma-vicaya* (intuitive investigation of phenomena), *ñāna* (level of insight) and *sammā-diṭṭhi* (right or clear understanding). As 'right understanding', wisdom is the first factor of the Eightfold Path. In the Buddha's teachings various forms and levels of wisdom are distinguished, which I will discuss below.

---

1 As a comparison: perception or *saññā*, the third universal mental factor described in chapter 8, is like a small child who recognises a PC as a computer, but who does not know anything else about it. The *citta*s from part 1 and part 2 can be compared to people who have a general knowledge of a computer and who are good at using it as a word processor, but who cannot use it for other purposes. Wisdom is like a computer programmer who has a full understanding of how a computer works. Through his experience of working with computers, he has developed a certain intuition so that he can recognise and solve problems before they become too serious.

Types of wisdom and insight

1. We reap what we sow

This insight refers to the deep-rooted realisation that we ourselves are responsible for all our actions, and that sooner or later we will experience the sweet or bitter fruits of these. This fundamental understanding, which is called *kammassakatā-sammā-diṭṭhi*, asks us to cultivate a healthy discernment between what is wholesome and what is not, so that we can see clearly and choose a path that leads to more happiness, insight and harmony. This insight lies at the root of walking a spiritual path, and it is the foundation of meditation practice.

2. Awareness

This, and the next forms of insight, can be realised through an awakening process that is initiated by the practice of insight meditation. First of all we become aware of experiences we were not aware of before. This second form of insight starts with the growing understanding that in fact we know very little about ourselves. A large part of our mental and physical experience seems to happen unconsciously, and we are controlled by those experiences in invisible ways. When practising insight meditation, gradually all kinds of mental and physical processes are 'charted'. Each moment of awareness regarding what is clearly happening in or to us in the here and now, is at the same time a moment of inner spaciousness. Whereas before we were caught up in thoughts, emotions and other experiences, now there is a liberating recognition of what is going on. This second process of awakening can be seen as a journey of discovery, and the liberation that comes as a result can be compared to the relief we may experience when we suddenly see a flicker of light while lost in a dark cave.

3. *Clear understanding of cause and effect*

As a direct result of this journey of discovery, clear comprehension begins to unfold in relation to the processes of cause and effect. We begin to distinguish all kinds of connections and conditioning patterns in the phenomena we become aware of. At this point we get in touch with inner blockages and unresolved emotions, and we get to know ourselves on a deeper level. This understanding is not a rational analysis of why we experience certain thoughts, emotions or feelings. We are not looking for the how and why of our experiences, but with the help of mindfulness, *kammic* connections spontaneously begin to show themselves. This can be very clarifying and revealing, and has a healing effect on our lives.

This third type of insight has not only therapeutic aspects but also empirical and scientific elements. Scientists strive for an accurate and objective study of, for example, biological or chemical phenomena. In the same way we notice how mental and physical experiences are continually interacting with each other. Without interference or taboos, we observe and register in detail what is appearing moment by moment; there is no need to judge or try to rationalise what we encounter. The insight that arises from the cultivation of mindfulness is intuitive in nature.

The second and third forms of insight usually flow naturally from one to the other. Together they could be called psychosomatic insight, because they reveal the relationships between physical and mental phenomena. A clear example of this insight happened during a retreat. An elderly lady reported during the daily individual feedback session (called an 'interview' in this meditation tradition) that she had been suffering for years from skin problems on her legs and arms. She could never understand the cause of this and had already consulted many specialists, but she had never been given satisfactory answers to her questions about the skin condition. During the interview she noticed how she could not say exactly what she meant. After the interview she went back to her room, feeling tense and powerless because of not being able to express herself in words. Suddenly she noticed that she was itchy and that she was scratching herself vigorously. She then realised that in fact she often felt itchy in moments of powerlessness, and that she scratched herself without being aware of it. When subsequently she sat down and started to meditate she could name or register not only the itch but also the powerlessness, the irritation and the frustration, as well as other emotional reactions. Seeing this connection between body and mind was a real eye opener for her; it was a discovery that gave her the option to be more alert in future and to gradually stop the habitual scratching.

4. Existential wisdom

At this level three natural laws or universal characteristics of human existence are clearly revealed, namely impermanence, unsatisfactoriness and uncontrollability.

– Impermanence (*anicca*): all mental and physical phenomena that are observed turn out to be impermanent. In the texts this is stated as follows: 'First not existing they arise, are present, then finally pass away again'. As meditators we become aware in a deep, intuitive way that everything is finite.[2]

– Unsatisfactoriness (*dukkha*): all worldly phenomena are a constant mental and physical burden, and therefore cannot be considered satisfactory. Some experiences or situations

---

2   Only the enlightenment experience and concepts are seen as permanent in the *Abhidhamma*.

are clearly not satisfying —for example war, hunger or illness. However, pleasant and neutral situations and phenomena are also viewed as unsatisfactory, due to their transient nature.

–   Uncontrollability (*anattā*): our inability to control or manipulate impermanent and unsatisfactory processes can be considered as uncontrollability or ungovernability. This last natural law also refers to the Buddhist concept of 'no-self'. In Buddhist psychology it is said that there is no ego, 'self' or solid identity that controls our lives. Life consists of countless mental and physical experiences that are connected through a process of cause and effect; this can be compared to a river, which in reality consists of millions and millions of water drops. The idea of a 'self' or an 'ego' arises through identification with what are ultimately impermanent and unsatisfactory processes, which we interpret as 'mine' or 'I'. Based on this delusion we try to manipulate and control the river of life, often in a very forced manner. Even though we may be able to steer the course of life in a certain direction, ultimately the mental and physical processes are impermanent and ungovernable.

This fourth type of wisdom, too, arises from concentrated mindfulness and is intuitive in nature. It is not connected with thought but based instead on a direct, clear awareness of what is happening here and now in body and mind. Clear comprehension of these three natural laws, which might be called existential wisdom, has various wholesome effects. A deeper understanding of impermanence results in a more flexible attitude in coping with the vicissitudes of life. There will be less fear of losing and of dying. The understanding of unsatifactoriness is fertile ground for greater tolerance, and for treating with compassion our own suffering and the suffering of others. Fully realising uncontrol-lability works as a cure for our tendency to (forcefully) try to manipulate uncontrollable situations in life. In this way existential insight leads to deeper happiness and well-being. The first four forms of wisdom remain in the mundane sphere, however.

5. *Transcendental wisdom*

The fifth and last form of wisdom can be realised on the basis of the previous types of wisdom. When the meditative pow-ers are sufficiently developed, ordinary worldly experience is transcended and supramundane types of consciousness will take place: path-consciousness and fruition-consciousness (see chapter 7). Both types of consciousness have *nibbāna* as their object; wisdom is clearly present as one of the mental factors. According to the Buddhist scriptures the Four Noble Truths are being fully penetrated. Suffering is completely understood. The cause of suffering is removed. The cessation of suffering is real-ised, and the Eightfold Path that leads to the end of suffering is fully cultivated.

The Four Noble Truths

The essence of the Buddha's teaching is contained in understand-ing the Four Noble Truths. The term 'truths' is used to indicate that it involves aspects of life that are irrefutable; facts, in other words. The word 'noble' indicates respect for these four truths, and a deep understanding of the Four Noble Truths leads to a pro-found and noble happiness. The Four Noble Truths are recognised by all schools of Buddhism and are considered the foundation of the Buddhist teachings. What follows is a concise explanation of these four truths.

1. There is suffering (dukkha-sacca)

As human beings we are confronted with pain and difficulties that are universal. We can experience poverty and hunger, or (incurable) illness, or we might find it difficult to grow older and cope with the physical limits that come with old age. Apart from these physical types of pain or discomfort we may also be confronted with mental pain, like the burning sensations of jealousy, fear, frustrations, unrequited love, bereavement, unfulfilled desires or loneliness.

The Buddha recognised this human vulnerability and formulated it as the first of the Four Noble Truths: 'there is suffering' (dukkha). The meaning of this Pali word can probably be rendered best as the unsatisfactory, unfulfilled, frustrating, burdensome, conflicting and painful nature of life.

This diagnosis of the nature of life itself is extremely profound. First of all we can suffer in a direct and very obvious way. All forms of physical and mental pain, as mentioned above, are included in this. But we also experience many pleasant moments in life. We may enjoy the fine weather in summer, or we may be appreciated for what we do. A long-cherished desire may be fulfilled, or we may experience feelings of joy for one reason or another. We do not immediately experience such moments as painful, yet in Buddhist psychology they are considered unsatisfactory, mainly because they are impermanent. For these pleasant experiences are not everlasting; sooner or later they will disappear. The more we have become attached to these feelings, the more pain we will experience when they have gone. This second type of dukkha is a hidden or less obvious form of suffering.[3]

---

3   And suppose that pleasant experiences would be permanent, after some time we would possibly get fed up with them too, and begin to see the relativity of these experiences.

There are also many experiences in life that are neither pleasant nor unpleasant, but neutral in character. Very simple moments, perhaps, of merely seeing, hearing or thinking, unaccompanied by (strong) pleasant or unpleasant feelings. These experiences too are called unsatisfactory, because they don't give us everlasting peace. Furthermore, they are a source of suffering when we are not aware of their presence or of their neutral character. This ignorance can easily result in dullness, apathy, boredom or uncertainty. It can be said that all wordly phenomena are ultimately unsatisfactory because of their impermanent and uncontrollable nature.

2. There is a cause of suffering (samudaya-sacca)

Just as an illness often has a cause—whether directly or indirectly—the Buddha discovered that the suffering we experience has a cause, namely desire or craving and the attachment that often follows from this. He mentioned three obvious forms of desire and attachment: sense desire, the desire to be or to become, and the desire to destroy.[4]

The *Abhidhamma* states that ultimately all problems arise from ignorance, the fourteenth mental factor discussed in chapter 9. Ignorance and delusion as regards pleasant sense stimuli cause desire and attachment. With unpleasant stimuli they lead to aversion, hatred, fear or jealousy, and with neutral stimuli to confusion, uncertainty, boredom or apathy. In this way we unconsciously create all kinds of habitual patterns that keep us in bondage and cause suffering.

---

4   The second Noble Truth refers to *cetasika* number 18. See chapter 2 and chapter 9 for more information about desire.

3. Cessation of suffering is possible (nirodha-sacca)

The Buddha once said: 'Oh monks, I teach only one thing: suffering and the cessation of suffering'.[5] According to the Buddha's teaching it is possible to come to the removal or cessation of suffering. In Pali the word *nirodha* is used in this context; it can be translated as 'no longer being imprisoned'. Chapter 7 has already discussed the purifying experience that is called enlightenment or *nibbāna*. This experience goes beyond all ordinary worldly experience and therefore cannot be described accurately. In the Buddhist scriptures the enlightenment experience is often approached by way of negations, explaining what it is *not*. However, *nibbāna* generally *is* described as a 'state of the highest peace and happiness' (*santi*), because it is disconnected from all (impermanent) worldly experience, as 'safe' (*khema*) or as 'liberating' (*vimutti*).

In the *Abhidhamma* the enlightenment experience refers to the fourth ultimate reality; this can be tasted with the supramundane types of consciousness described in chapter 7 and the transcendental level of insight mentioned above.

4. There is a way leading to the cessation of suffering (magga-sacca)

The fourth Noble Truth can be seen as a guide to *Dhamma* practice; it is called the Eightfold Path. This path can be compared to a natural remedy that is composed of eight ingredients or guidelines that together result in the ending of suffering. Walking or practising the Eightfold Path can be done at various levels. First of all, the Eightfold Path is diagnostic and shows problems and limitations. Furthermore, it leads to quicker and better acceptance

---

5   The Buddha possibly combined suffering and the cessation of suffering because the ending of suffering can only be realised when we experience suffering. They are inextricably bound up with each other.

of these. It also has a healing effect, because following the eight-fold path results in the alleviation and ultimately the complete ending of human suffering. Below I will reflect briefly on the different aspects of the Eightfold Path, which is composed of eight mental factors.

1. Right view (*sammā-diṭṭhi*). First of all this refers to the first type of insight discussed in this chapter, namely the discernment of what is wholesome and what is not. This wisdom allows us to find a way that leads to more happiness, insight and harmony. From this basic insight we can cultivate wholesome thoughts and ideas, which then constitute the next factor of the Eightfold Path.

2. Right thought (*sammā-sankappa*). In the Buddha's teachings we are advised to cultivate three types of thoughts, namely thoughts renouncing (sensual) desire and attachment, thoughts not rooted in hatred or anger, and thoughts that are free from resentment. A simple example of developing right thought is the decision to smoke less or drink less when you notice that tobacco or alcohol affects you badly. Other examples are seeing the good in people, being open to the suffering of others and practising meditation on loving kindness.[6] Right thought refers to the wholesome aspect of *vitakka*, the eighth mental factor described in chapter 8.

The first two factors of the Eightfold Path are aspects of wisdom; the next three are connected with ethical behaviour or morality. These factors concern the three abstinences mentioned in the previous chapter.

---

6   See chapter 11.

3. Right speech (*sammā-vācā*). The advice connected with right speech is to refrain from telling lies, from gossiping, cursing or talking nonsense, particularly when it may cause unnecessary confusion, pain or sorrow.

4. Right action (*sammā-kammanta*). This fourth guideline is the advice to refrain from actions that cause disharmony and are (self-)destructive. Examples are killing, stealing, violent or abusive sexual conduct, and using alcohol or drugs (to the degree that it affects clarity of mind).

5. Right livelihood (*sammā-ājīva*). This guideline is the advice to refrain from hurting ourselves and others in our jobs, hobbies or other day-to-day activities. Examples are selling weapons, dealing in drugs, committing fraud or having a job that involves killing or inciting others to kill.

The sixth, seventh and eighth factors of the Eightfold Path relate to how we deal with actions, thoughts and emotions on an inner level. They are largely developed through meditation.

6. Right effort (*sammā-vāyāma*). Right effort is the eleventh mental factor mentioned in chapter 8: *viriya*. It refers to the balanced effort to not provide fuel for unwholesome or unskilful thoughts and emotions, and to stop them. Furthermore, we develop right effort when we cultivate and nourish wholesome deeds and emotions.

7. Right mindfulness (*sammā-sati*). Right mindfulness—mental factor number 29, described in chapter 10—is the power of observation with regard to what is happening in or around us in the present moment. It is an open and attentive

awareness of body, feelings, thoughts, sense impressions and emotions in the here and now.

8. Right concentration (*sammā-samādhi*). The eighth and last aspect of the Eightfold Path is one-pointedness of mind: mental factor number 5, mentioned in chapter 8.

All factors of the Eightfold Path are called *right* (*sammā*). By right (or correct) is meant 'in accordance with the aim of following the Eightfold Path, namely developing wisdom and harmony, and ending our suffering'. It also indicates a balance or (meditative) equilibrium. If, for example, we develop the sixth or the eighth factor of the Eightfold Path too much or too little, other aspects may be (temporarily) blocked. The eight guidelines of the path are connected, and they act like an upward spiral: the development of one aspect promotes the next one. The Eightfold Path can be considered the practical way *and* the process of awakening that leads to realising all aspects of insight as described in this chapter.

Insight and the eightfold path

The Eightfold Path can be most fully realised by developing mindfulness, which is the essence of practising insight meditation. Based on the first type of insight, right understanding, we begin to walk the spiritual path, and we start to cultivate mindfulness. Right thought, the second aspect of the Eightfold Path, is manifested as getting in touch with or becoming aware of the physical or mental experience that is predominant in the moment. In naming or noting what is experienced right speech is realised, for in that moment we do not tell lies, gossip or curse; neither do we talk nonsense, because we observe and name things as they are. Right action and right livelihood are observed by occupying ourselves with a harmless and kind activity, namely the practice of meditation.

Right effort is the balanced effort with which we observe and register. From this arises and grows the power of right mindfulness. As a direct result of a moment of mindfulness we develop a deeper, natural focus on the experiences we are aware of. From this right concentration deeper forms of right or clear insight are revealed, as was discussed at the beginning of this chapter. This automatically reinforces inner discipline and ethical sensitivity. Energy and effort increase and become more balanced with right mindfulness; concentration in turn becomes sharper, insight or right understanding deepens again, and so on. In this way the aspects of the Eightfold Path are developed more and more. The Buddha compared this process to a wheel with eight spokes; this wheel is set in motion by the practice of meditation and runs more and more smoothly as we continue to practise. In doing so we pass through all the different types of insight until the highest liberating insight is realised, crowning the process of meditation.

All these forms of insight are not theoretical or intellectual, but intuitive in nature. This wisdom proves to be very useful in daily life; therefore it can be seen as a valuable friend. It offers protection from forces like desire, hatred and ignorance, which lead to suffering. It is the key to self-knowledge, to how we can use skilful means to achieve desired results, and to how we can manage the ups and downs of life in a wise and skilful manner. Wisdom works preventatively, because intuitively we can more easily pick up signs of possible danger, and we begin to understand how we may prevent, get round or creatively solve problems. In short, wisdom leads to happiness and freedom.

PART FOUR

PSYCHOLOGICAL ANALYSES

The previous parts of this book described all the types of consciousness and their concomitants. This part looks at the relationships between consciousness and the mental factors. Chapter 13 discusses two kinds of combinations: (1) with which type of consciousness can the various mental factors associate, and (2) with which mental factors can the various types of consciousness arise. Some explicit themes in our psychic functioning will then be illustrated to show in more detail how consciousness works. Chapter 14 describes feelings and root causes, while chapter 15 deals with functions and doors.

To help their students get more familiar with these subjects, Southeast Asian *Abhidhamma* schools give them assignments. For the reader who likes puzzles I have included a number of these assignments; the answers can be found in the footnotes.

Warning: part 4 may seem somewhat tedious because of the various figures and combinations. This part of the book, therefore, is aimed at readers who are particularly interested in the finer points of the *Abhidhamma*.

13

THE ASSOCIATIONS AND COMBINATIONS OF CONSCIOUSNESS AND ITS MENTAL FACTORS

Part 1, part 2 and part 3 have described the two important aspects of the mind, namely consciousness—with its function of knowing an object—and the mental factors—which all perform a specific function with regard to consciousness. Although when explaining consciousness and the mental factors I have separated them, in practical terms they cannot exist without each other. Just as hydrogen and oxygen together constitute water, so the combination of *cittas* and *cetasikas* is what constitutes our psyche. To enable us to penetrate more deeply into the theory, I would like to describe these connections for the motivated reader by way of two forms of combinations:

1. With which types of consciousness can the various mental factors arise?
2. With which mental factors can the various types of consciousness arise?

1. With which types of consciousness can the various mental factors associate (*sampayoganaya*)?

The *Abhidhamma* describes consistently and in great detail the types of consciousness with which the mental factors can associate. In that sense it may look like a contemporary model of mathematical formulas. See below for the table with an explanation.

Table 13.1

Explanation: The circles are the mental factors. The numbers in these circles are the types of consciousness with which the mental factor concerned may arise.

– Seven universal

(121) (121) (121) (121) (121) (121) (121)

– Six occasional

(55) (66) (110) (105) (51) (101)

– Four with ignorance

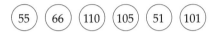

(12) (12) (12) (2)

– Three with desire

(8) (4) (4)

– Four with aversion

(2) (2) (2) (2)

– Two with drowsiness

(5) (5)

- One doubt

- Nineteen universal wholesome

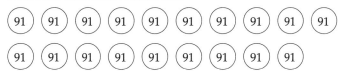

- Three abstinences

- Two illimitables

- One wisdom

1–7. The seven universal mental factors arise with all one hundred and twenty-one types of consciousness (121).

8. Initial application (*vitakka*) can be found with fifty-five *citta*s, namely with the twelve unwholesome *citta*s, with eight of the eighteen rootless types of *citta* (not with the ten rootless sense *citta*s), with the twenty-four wholesome types of consciousness, with the three types of consciousness of the first fine-material absorption, and with the eight types of consciousness of the first supramundane absorption (12 + 8 + 24 + 3 + 8 = 55).

9. Sustained application (*vicāra*) can be found with sixty-six types of consciousness, namely with the fifty-five types of *vitakka* and the eleven types of consciousness of the second (fine-material and supramundane) *jhānas* (55 + 3 + 8 = 66).

10. Decision (*adhimokkha*) can be found with one hundred and ten types of consciousness, and is not associated with the eleventh unwholesome type of consciousness (doubt), and not with the ten rootless types of sense consciousness either (11 + 8 + 24 + 27 + 40 = 110).

11. Effort (*viriya*) can be found with all unwholesome, wholesome, fine-material, immaterial and supramundane *cittas*. With regard to rootless *cittas*, effort only arises with the mind-door adverting consciousness and with the smile-producing-consciousness (12 + 2 + 24 + 27 + 40 = 105).

12. Joy (*pīti*) arises with all types of consciousness with a pleasant feeling. These are the first four unwholesome *cittas*, the investigating *citta* that is accompanied by pleasant feeling, the smile-producing-consciousness, the first four active wholesome, the first four resultant wholesome and the first four functional wholesome *cittas*, and the types of consciousness of the first three (fine-material and supramundane absorptions) (4 + 2 + 12 + 11 + 11 + 11 = 51).

13. Wish (*chanda*) is present with all types of consciousness, except with the rootless *cittas* and with the last two unwholesome types of consciousness, with doubt and with restlessness (10 + 24 + 27 + 40 = 101).

14–17. The four universal unwholesome mental factors, which have ignorance as their leader, only arise with the twelve unwholesome types of consciousness (12).

18. Desire or greed (*lobha*) arises with the eight types of consciousness that are rooted in desire or attachment (8).

19. Wrong view (*diṭṭhi*) arises mainly with the four unwholesome types of consciousness that are rooted in desire or attachment and that are accompanied by wrong view (4).

20. Conceit or pride (*māna*) also arises with four of the eight unwholesome types of consciousness with desire, but particularly with the four other than those with wrong view. According to the *Abhidhamma* conceit and wrong view can never arise at the same time; they are two different expressions of desire (4).[1]

21–24. The four mental factors with hatred as their leader are associated with the two hateful types of consciousness (2).

25 and 26. The two mental factors with drowsiness as their leader arise with the five prompted unwholesome types of consciousness (four with attachment and one with hatred). The prompted unwholesome types of consciousness are less powerful, so laziness and drowsiness can easily come about (4 + 1 = 5).

27. Doubt (*vicikicchā*)—the last unwholesome factor—arises only with the eleventh unwholesome type of consciousness (1).

---

1   See chapter 9 for more details.

28–46. The nineteen universal wholesome or 'universal beautiful' mental factors always arise spontaneously with all wholesome types of consciousness—that is, with the twenty-four wholesome types of consciousness, the twenty-seven fine-material and immaterial types of consciousness and the forty supramundane types of consciousness (24 + 27 + 40 = 91).

47–49. The three abstinences can occasionally arise with the eight active wholesome types of consciousness, and they always arise with the forty supramundane types of consciousness (8 + 40 = 48).

50 and 51. The two illimitables (compassion and sympathetic joy) can occasionally arise with the eight active wholesome and with the eight functional wholesome types of consciousness. They can also arise with the twelve types of consciousness of the first four fine-material *jhāna*s, when compassion or sympathetic joy is the object of concentration. The fifth fine-material *jhāna*s cannot be realised through meditation on compassion and sympathetic joy. The reason is that compassion and sympathetic joy are automatically accompanied by pleasant feeling while the last fine-material absorption and the immaterial absorptions are always accompanied by neutral feeling (8 + 8 + 12 = 28).[2]

52. Wisdom always arises with the twelve wholesome types of consciousness associated with insight; it also arises with all sublime and supramundane *citta*s (12 + 27 + 40 = 79).[3]

---

2   Compassion and sympathetic joy do not automatically arise with these types of consciousness. Only when the right conditions are present do they arise. A social worker will have more opportunities and inner space for compassion, while a soldier might find it more difficult to get in touch with compassion.

3   There is *jhāna-sammā-diṭṭhi* in the twenty-seven sublime types of consciousness. This is a lighter form of insight with which we realise that a special mental state is present.

EXCURSION: Drowsiness during the practice of meditation

For most meditators drowsiness or sleepiness is a familiar experience. I was struggling with it for a long time, and even now I am regularly faced with it while meditating. In *Liberating Insight* (Silkworm Books, 2004) I outlined a number of causes of sleepiness and gave hints on how to work with it. But how exactly do drowsiness and lethargy arise in a psychological sense? And how is it that—according to the *Abhidhamma*, as shown above—drowsiness arises particularly with the five prompted unwholesome types of consciousness? I answer these questions in the following way:

– In daily life we are often quite busy with doing and with achieving. We live and act from willpower or *cetanā* (the fourth universal mental factor) and are often using a lot of effort (mental factor number 11) in what we do. After having exerted effort for a long time, the mental vitality or *jīvitindriya* (universal concomitant number 6) diminishes, but we continue to live on willpower. During the practice of insight meditation we emphasise more the art of being with what is. And when we have pleasant experiences and begin to feel calm and peaceful, we easily forget (to continue) to name or note this objectively. The result is that mental cognitive processes arise, where unwholesome *citta*s accompanied by desire or attachment play an important part as scanning consciousness. We are mostly not aware of this. And because the mental factors of willpower and effort are not strong we usually experience prompted unwholesome types of consciousness, which are less stimulating and forceful than types of consciousness that are unprompted. Sluggishness and lethargy can therefore easily infiltrate and we sink into drowsiness.

— Meditators often tell me that they feel that they might become sleepy because of not wanting to experience something, or that they even unconsciously push something away. This can easily happen. For when we experience something unpleasant—like pain, or unwelcome thoughts or emotions—we (unconsciously) would rather not feel them. In these moments arise the prompted type of consciousness with hatred as its leader, and because this doesn't feel good drowsiness and lethargy accompany this scanning consciousness as discouraging factors: we bury our head in the sand.

For many meditators sleepiness is one of the most difficult meditation objects, particularly because we tend to get overwhelmed by it and then it is difficult to recognise. Practice, however, makes perfect. From the above-mentioned principle it can be concluded that we may prevent sleepiness by carefully beginning to observe and note pleasant and unpleasant feelings. When sleepiness arises all the same, being aware in an allowing way and noting it with non-identification usually work quite well, particularly when someone is already trained in mindfulness practice. Then we may consider sleepiness or drowsiness as a (valuable) meditation object, where we allow the sleepiness to be present while at the same time we try to note or register it when it is predominant. In this way we can note or name laziness, dullness, sleepiness, lethargy, and feeling light, 'woolly', heavy or tired as meditation experiences. Yawning, nodding off or whatever other symptoms may be predominant, we can use them as meditation objects and note them.

This may not always be possible, however. To conclude this excursion I would like to quote a passage from the *Anguttara Nikāya* (the Numerical Discourses of the Buddha) in which the

Buddha gives his student Moggallāna additional guidelines on how to deal with persistent drowsiness.

The Blessed One said to the Venerable Moggallāna:

'Are you nodding, Moggallāna?' 'Yes, Lord.'
    'Well then, Moggallāna, at whatever thought drowsiness befalls you, you should give attention to that thought. Then, by doing so, it is possible that your drowsiness will vanish.
    But if, by doing so, your drowsiness does not vanish, then you should ponder the *Dhamma* as you have learnt it and mastered it, you should examine it and investigate it closely in your mind. Then, by doing so, it is possible …
    But if, by doing so, your drowsiness does not vanish, then you should recite in detail the *Dhamma* as you have learnt it and mastered it. Then, by doing so it is possible …
    But if, by doing so, your drowsiness does not vanish, then you should pull both earlobes and rub your limbs with your hands. Then, by doing so, it is possible …
    But if, by doing so, your drowsiness does not vanish, you should get up from your seat and, after washing your eyes with water, you should look around in all directions and upwards to the stars and constellations. Then, by doing so, it is possible …
    But if, by doing so, your drowsiness does not vanish, then you should attend to the perception of light, resolve upon the perception of daytime: as by day, so at night; as at night, so by day. Thus, with an open and unencumbered heart, you should develop a luminous mind. Then, by doing so, it is possible …

But if, by doing so, your drowsiness does not vanish, then, with your senses turned inward and your mind not straying outward, you should take to walking up and down, being aware of going to and fro. Then, by doing so, it is possible ...

But if, by doing so, your drowsiness does not vanish, then, mindful and clearly comprehending, you may lie down, lion-like, on your right side, placing one foot on the other, keeping in mind the thought of rising; and on awaking, you should quickly get up, thinking: "I must not indulge in the pleasure of resting and reclining, in the pleasure of sleep."

Thus, Moggallāna, you should train yourself.' (AN 7.58)

2. With which mental factors can the various types of consciousness combine (*sangahanaya*)?

This analysis is exactly the other way around. Now the *citta*s are the point of departure and we look at which *cetasika*s (can) arise with them.

Table 13.2

Explanation: The circles are the types of consciousness. The figures in these circles are the mental factors with which the respective type of consciousness can combine.

– Twelve unwholesome

(19) (21) (19) (21)

(18) (20) (18) (20)

(20) (22)

(15) (15)

– Eighteen rootless

(7) (7) (7) (7) (7)   (10) (10)

(7) (7) (7) (7) (7)   (10) (10)   (11)

(10) (11) (12)

– Twenty-four wholesome

(38) (38) (37) (37)

(37) (37) (36) (36)

(33) (33) (32) (32)

(32) (32) (31) (31)

(35) (35) (34) (34)

(34) (34) (33) (33)

– Fifteen fine-material + Twelve immaterial

(35) (34) (33) (32) (30)

(35) (34) (33) (32) (30)

(35) (34) (33) (32) (30)

(30) (30) (30) (30)

(30) (30) (30) (30)

(30) (30) (30) (30)

– Forty supramundane

(36) (35) (34) (33) (33)

(36) (35) (34) (33) (33)

(36) (35) (34) (33) (33)

(36) (35) (34) (33) (33)

(36) (35) (34) (33) (33)

(36) (35) (34) (33) (33)

(36) (35) (34) (33) (33)

(36) (35) (34) (33) (33)

Twelve unwholesome types of consciousness

The first type of unwholesome consciousness is spontaneous or unprompted; it is accompanied by pleasant feeling and is associated with wrong view. With this *citta* nineteen mental factors arise, namely the first thirteen concomitants, the four universal unwholesome concomitants, desire and wrong view (13 + 4 + 2 = 19).

The second type of unwholesome consciousness arises after prompting and is accompanied by pleasant feeling; it is associated with wrong view. With this *citta* twenty-one mental factors arise, namely the same nineteen factors as above; because it concerns a *citta* that is not spontaneous, drowsiness and lethargy may also arise (13 + 4 + 2 + 2 = 21).

The third type of consciousness is unprompted and arises with pleasant feeling, but is not associated with wrong view. The same nineteen mental factors as in number one arise, except that now wrong view is replaced with conceit (13 + 4 + 2 = 19).

In a similar way the *cetasika*s of the fourth type of unwholesome consciousness are the same as of number two, and wrong view is again replaced with conceit (13 + 4 + 2 + 2 = 21).

The fifth to eighth types of unwholesome consciousness correspond to the first four unwholesome *citta*s, except that they are without joy, because they are accompanied by neutral feeling instead of pleasant feeling (18, 20, 18 and 20).

The ninth type of unwholesome consciousness is rooted in hatred and is unprompted. Twelve of the first thirteen mental factors associate with this type of consciousness; the exception again is joy, for this type of consciousness concerns a *citta* with unpleasant feeling. In addition, the four universal unwholesome concomitants arise and there is also scope for the arising of the four mental factors with hatred as their leader. In total this comes to twenty mental factors. Of these, jealousy, stinginess and remorse are optional, and they arise independently of one another according to the situation. The other mental factors always arise (12 + 4 + 4 = 20).

With the tenth *citta* twenty-two mental factors arise, namely the twenty *cetasika*s of number 9, and in addition drowsiness and lethargy; for it concerns a *citta* that is prompted (12 + 4 + 4 + 2 = 22).

With the eleventh type of consciousness, which is associated with doubt, fifteen *cetasika*s arise, namely the seven universal mental factors, *vitakka*, *vicāra*, effort, the four universal unwholesome concomitants and doubt. Absent are decision (for there is hesitation or doubt), joy and the wish to do (7 + 3 + 4 + 1= 15).

With the twelfth and last unwholesome type of consciousness there are also fifteen *cetasika*s present. However in this case doubt is replaced with decision (7 + 3 + 4 + 1 = 15).

Eighteen rootless types of consciousness

The ten rootless types of sense consciousness, namely five as the result of unwholesome *kamma* and five as the result of wholesome *kamma*, have only seven concomitants, namely the seven universal mental factors. For the sake of clarity they have been circled with a dotted line (7).

The two receiving *citta*s, the two investigating *citta*s and the five sense-door adverting *citta*s are all five accompanied by neutral feeling and have ten concomitants, namely the seven universal mental factors, *vitakka*, *vicāra*, and decision (7 + 3 = 10)

The investigating *citta* that is accompanied by pleasant feeling also has joy as its concomitant (7 + 3 + 1 = 11).

The mind-door adverting *citta*, accompanied by neutral feeling (the seventeenth rootless type of consciousness), is associated with eleven concomitants, namely the seven universal mental factors, *vitakka*, *vicāra*, decision and effort (7 + 4 = 11).

With the last rootless *citta*, smile-producing-consciousness, joy is added to these factors and it is therefore associated with twelve mental factors (7 + 5 = 12).

Twenty-four wholesome types of consciousness

The first two active wholesome types of consciousness are associ-ated with thirty-eight mental factors, namely the seven universal *cetasika*s, the six occasional and the twenty-five wholesome or beautiful factors. Of these, one of the three abstinences or one of the two illimitables arise only when the right conditions are present. The other mental factors always arise (7 + 6 + 19 + 3 + 2 + 1 = 38).

The third and fourth active wholesome types of consciousness are associated with thirty-seven concomitants, namely those men-tioned above, with the exception of wisdom (7+ 6 + 19 + 3 + 2 = 37).

The fifth and sixth *citta*s too arise with thirty-seven concomitants. In this case wisdom *is* present but joy is not, for it concerns *citta*s with neutral feeling (7 + 5 + 19 + 3 + 2 + 1 = 37).

In the last two active wholesome *citta*s wisdom is absent, so there are thirty-six mental factors ($7 + 6 + 19 + 3 + 2 = 36$).

Then there are eight wholesome types of consciousness as fruit or result. The first two of these *citta*s have thirty-three mental factors, namely the seven universal *cetasika*s, the six occasional *cetasika*s, the nineteen universal beautiful or wholesome *cetasika*s, and wisdom. The three abstinences and the two illimitables do not arise. For in this case it involves resultant *citta*s, while the three abstinences and the two illimitables can only be developed actively ($7 + 6 + 19 + 1 = 33$).

With the third and the fourth wholesome *vipāka-citta*s wisdom is absent ($7 + 6 + 19 = 32$).

With the fifth and sixth *citta*s wisdom *is* present, as a result of previously committed wholesome *kamma*, but there is no joy ($7 + 5 + 19 + 1 = 32$).

The seventh and eighth resultant types of consciousness are associated with only thirty-one concomitants, namely the seven universal mental factors, five of the six occasional *cetasika*s—joy is not present—and the nineteen universal wholesome mental factors ($7 + 5 + 19 = 31$).

The last eight wholesome *citta*s are functional, and they are experienced only by *arahat*s. With the first two functional wholesome *citta*s thirty-five mental factors can arise. The seven universal, the six occasional, the nineteen universal wholesome, and wisdom all arise automatically. When the conditions are appropriate compassion or sympathetic joy can also arise. The three abstinences are not experienced by an *arahat* because there is no longer the tendency for unwholesome *kamma* ($7 + 6 + 19 + 2 + 1 = 35$).

CONSCIOUSNESS AND ITS MENTAL FACTORS | 159

In the following two functional wholesome *cittas* wisdom is not present (7 + 6 + 19 + 2 = 34).

In the fifth and sixth wholesome *cittas* wisdom *is* present, but there is no joy, and with the last two functional wholesome *cittas* wisdom is again absent (34 and 33).

Twenty-seven sublime types of consciousness

The *cittas* of the first fine-material *jhāna* are associated with thirty-five concomitants. The seven universal, six occasional and nineteen universal wholesome mental factors, along with wisdom, arise automatically. When compassion or sympathetic joy was chosen as the meditation object then one of these two illimitables can arise as well (7 + 6 + 19 + 2 + 1 = 35).

In the types of consciousness of the second *jhāna vitakka* falls away (7 + 5 + 19 + 2 + 1 = 34).

In the third fine-material *jhāna-cittas vicāra* is no longer present either (7 + 4 + 19 + 2 + 1 = 33).

In the fourth absorption there is no joy (*pīti*) either (7 + 3 + 19 + 2 + 1 = 32).

In the fifth fine-material *jhāna* and in the twelve immaterial *jhāna-cittas* there cannot be compassion or sympathetic joy. These two illimitables are always accompanied by pleasant feeling and therefore can be developed only in the absorption levels with pleasant feeling. In the lower *jhānas* equanimity was in the background playing a balancing role. In the fifth *jhāna-citta*, however, it becomes clearly present and has developed into a dominant factor (7 + 3 + 19 + 1 = 30).

Forty supramundane types of consciousness

Finally, there are the forty *citta*s that are involved in the experience of enlightenment. Arising in the four forms of path consciousness and fruition consciousness of the first supramundane absorption are thirty-six *cetasika*s, namely the seven universal *cetasika*s, the six occasional and the nineteen universal wholesome mental factors, the three abstinences and wisdom. The three abstinences arise simultaneously, because the Eightfold Path is now fully present and the tendency towards unwholesome speech, actions and livelihood has been completely eradicated (7 + 6 + 19 + 3 + 1 = 36).

The way of counting continues according to the realisations through the *jhāna*s.

In the subsequent supramundane absorptions, just as in the fine-material and immaterial absorptions, *vitakka*, *vicāra* and joy fall away in sequence (35, 34 and 33).

14

FEELINGS AND ROOT CAUSES

Feelings

Table 14.1: Feelings

Explanation: The numbers in the types of consciousness have the following meaning: '1' means that there is physical pleasant feeling, '2' means physical unpleasant feeling, '3' means mental pleasant feeling, '4' means mental unpleasant feeling, and '5' means mental neutral feeling.

– Twelve unwholesome

– Eighteen rootless

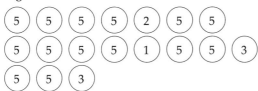

– Twenty-four wholesome

(3) (3) (3) (3)
(5) (5) (5) (5)

(3) (3) (3) (3)
(5) (5) (5) (5)

(3) (3) (3) (3)
(5) (5) (5) (5)

– Twenty-seven sublime

(3) (3) (3) (3) (5)
(3) (3) (3) (3) (5)
(3) (3) (3) (3) (5)

(5) (5) (5) (5)
(5) (5) (5) (5)
(5) (5) (5) (5)

– Forty supramundane

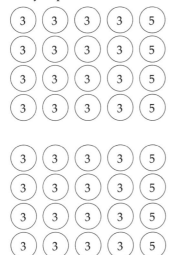

According to the *Abhidhamma*, feeling or *vedanā*—the second universal mental factor—plays an extremely important role in our lives. Feeling 'tastes' the object and knows five 'tastes':

1. Physical pleasant feeling (*sukha-vedanā*) experiences a pleasant tangible or physical object. It affects the other mental factors as pleasantly stimulating and reinforces them, and it is expressed as physical pleasure. One *citta* is accompanied by pleasant physical feeling, namely body-consciousness as the result of wholesome *kamma*.

2. Physical unpleasant feeling (*dukkha-vedanā*) experiences an unpleasant tangible or physical object and affects the other mental factors in a destructive way. It is expressed as physical pain or an uncomfortable feeling in our body. This feeling too only arises with one *citta*, namely body-consciousness as

the result of unwholesome *kamma*.[1] The fact that physical feeling only arises with two *cittas* does not, however, mean that it is rarely present. Because physical feelings are grosser in character than mental feelings (which will be discussed below) we often experience these two *cittas* in our daily lives.

3. Mental pleasant feeling (*somanassa-vedanā*) or joy experiences a pleasant mental object. It participates in or enjoys the pleasant aspect of the object and is expressed as mental well-being. In meditation it is the result of calmness. Sixty-two types of consciousness are associated with a pleasant mental feeling, namely the first four unwholesome types of consciousness with desire, investigating-consciousness as the result of wholesome *kamma* in the past and accompanied by pleasant feeling, smile-producing-consciousness, the first four active, resultant and functional wholesome types of consciousness, and all fine-material and supramundane *cittas* from the first to the fourth absorptions (4 + 1 + 1 + 4 + 4 + 4 + 44 = 62)

4. Mental unpleasant feeling (*domanassa-vedanā*) experiences an unpleasant object. It 'consumes' the unpleasant aspect of this object and manifests as mental suffering. Only two types of consciousness are accompanied by an unpleasant mental feeling, namely the two unwholesome types of consciousness that are rooted in hatred or aversion.

5. Neutral mental feeling (*upekkhā-vedanā*) experiences the object as neutral. It is neither pleasant nor unpleasant, and

---

1   It is good to realise that there are also other causes for physical unpleasant feelings, such as temperature and food. See chapter 16 for more details.

it manifests as peacefulness. It is caused by consciousness without enthusiasm. All other *cittas* that are not mentioned above associate with neutral feeling.

Root causes

The second classification of consciousness is by way of roots or root causes (*hetus* in Pali). Just as the roots of a tree give strength and stability to the tree, so too six of the fifty-two concomitants give special strength and stability to the *cittas* and the other *cetasikas*. These mental factors also define the ethical aspect of consciousness. The following six root causes are mentioned:

1. Desire or greed (*lobha*). Desire grasps an object and attaches itself to it. Desire manifests as clinging, just like a pitbull terrier clings to its prey (see chapter 9, mental factor number 18). Its proximate cause is seeing pleasure or happiness in things that in reality only result in addiction or dependence. Desire and the resulting attachment are present in the first eight unwholesome types of consciousness.

2. Hatred or aversion (*dosa*) (see chapter 9, mental factor number 21). Hatred can be found with the two unwholesome types of consciousness that are accompanied by hatred.

3. Ignorance (*moha*). Delusion or ignorance is the mental poverty or blindness that prevents us from seeing clearly what is happening in and to us at any moment. Ignorance can also manifest as covering up or not facing reality. Ignorance can be found with all twelve types of unwholesome consciousness. The first three roots are, ethically speaking, unwholesome in character because they increase suffering

and prevent deeper happiness. They can be called the three destructive roots.

4. Generosity or non-attachment (*alobha*). *Alobha* is the wholesome opposite of desire and does not have any self-serving interest in the object that is perceived, and it does not appropriate this object. It manifests as non-attachment. *Alobha* has, as described in chapter 10, a passive and an active manifestation, namely as non-desire, as unselfishness or as generosity. The passive form is an unobtrusive mental factor with the resultant and functional wholesome, fine-material, immaterial and supramundane types of consciousness. As an active root it manifests as generosity with the active wholesome types of consciousness. *Alobha* arises with ninety-one *cittas*.

5. Benevolence or non-hatred (*adosa*). The characteristics of *adosa* are not being hateful and non-resentment. *Adosa* too has a passive and an active aspect. The passive manifestation is again an unobtrusive but wholesome participant in consciousness and its concomitants. As an active root, *adosa* manifests as benevolence or as loving kindness. It arises with the same ninety-one types of consciousness as *alobha*.

6. Wisdom or non-delusion (*amoha*). Wisdom investigates and penetrates the reality of phenomena. It throws light in the dark, creates clarity and is the opposite of wrong view, delusion or ignorance. *Amoha*—literally meaning absence of delusion—has only one manifestation, namely wisdom. Wisdom arises with seventy-nine types of consciousness, namely the twelve wholesome types of consciousness associated with wisdom and all the fine-material, immaterial and supramundane types of consciousness. The last three

root causes are, ethically speaking, wholesome and con-structive in character.[2]

ASSIGNMENT
....
Investigate which root causes can be found with the different types of consciousness.

....

EXCURSION: Three healing powers
....

The underlying principles of Buddhist psychology are positive. Although suffering plays an important part as the basis of exis-tence, much attention is given to the happiness we can experience when we follow a spiritual path. This profound happiness is fur-ther illustrated in table 14.3 by way of a detailed description of the three wholesome powers *alobha*, *adosa* and *amoha* (mental factors number 32, 33 and 34 as described in part 3). These three powers are the opposites of the afflictive or destructive roots of desire, hatred and ignorance. The way in which the *Abhidhamma* analyses these three healing powers is, in my view, quite illuminating, and table 14.3 below shows this analysis.

....

---

2   It is curious that the last three powers are described in negative forms as non-desire, non-hatred and non-delusion. The reason for this is probably that the Buddha stated that the absence of desire, hatred and ignorance is already extremely wholesome.

Table 14.3

ALOBHA	ADOSA	AMOHA
The absence of desire	The absence of hatred	The absence of delusion
Is the opposite of self-ishness and greed	Is the opposite of hatred and unwholesomeness	Is the opposite of ignorance and of not cultivating wholesome conditions
Is the cause of generosity	Is the cause of virtue	Is the cause of meditation
Causes us not to eat too much	Causes us not to eat too little	Causes us not to eat what is spoiled
Causes us to face and admit our mistakes	Causes us to recognise virtues	Causes us to see and acknowledge reality as it is
Causes us not to feel sad when we have to be separated from what is dear to us	Causes us not to be sad when we are in contact with pain or something unpleasant	Causes us not to be sad when we cannot get what we want
Causes us not to feel mental pain when change happens	Causes us not to feel mental pain when we get old or ill	Causes us not to feel mental pain when we die
Creates a harmonious way of life for lay people	Creates a harmonious way of life for all people	Creates a harmonious way of life for monastics
Causes us not to get frustrated	Causes us not to experience life as hellish	Causes us to live and die without confusion and fear
Prevents us from approaching something or someone out of desire	Prevents us from approaching something or someone out of hatred or aversion	Prevents us approaching something or someone out of indifference
Prevents addiction and overindulgence	Prevents self-mortification and strictness, and softens a negative self-image	Ensures a balanced middle way between the two extremes

Table 14.3 (continued)

ALOBHA	ADOSA	AMOHA
Brings about the absence of greed and attachment	Brings about the absence of ill will	Brings about the absence of superstition and dogmatism
Provides a gateway to mindfulness of body and feelings	Provides a gateway to mindfulness of body and feelings	Provides a gateway to mindfulness of thinking and mental states
Gives good health	Gives radiance	Gives long life
Leads to wealth	Leads to having good friends	Leads to dealing with stress and difficulties wisely
Leads to rebirth in one of the seven heavenly realms of Buddhist cosmology	Leads to rebirth in one of the sixteen fine-material or in one of the four immaterial realms	Leads to enlightenment
Causes us to be not afraid of losing our wealth	Causes us to live easily in a difficult situation	Causes us to deal skilfully with neutral periods in our life
Offers insight into the impermanence of all phenomena	Offers insight into suffering	Offers insight into the uncontrollable and 'selfless' nature of all phenomena
Insight into impermanence (*anicca*) leads to the absence of attachment and desire	Insight into suffering (*dukkha*) leads to the absence of hatred	Insight into uncontrollability (*anattā*) leads to wisdom
Is developed as a healing power in every moment of mindfulness	Is developed as a healing power in every moment of mindfulness	Is developed as a healing power in every moment of mindfulness

15

FUNCTIONS AND DOORS

Functions

Part 1 and part 2 described one hundred and twenty-one differ-ent types of consciousness; for clarity they have been depicted again below (table 15.1). To make the picture of how our mind works even more complete we need to know that *citta*s can have different functions (some *citta*s even perform four or five differ-ent functions). This can be compared to a village in which live one hundred and twenty-one people. All of them have their own unique personality and are called, for example, John, Peter or Mary. John performs different tasks and functions. He may be known as a carpenter, but in the evenings he is called a husband and a father. Sometimes he helps others, sometimes he's a par-tygoer, and so on. In the same way, types of consciousness can perform fourteen functions, which are described below.

1. Rebirth. In chapter 4 I described rebirth. Only once in our life, namely at the time of conception, does *citta* have the function of rebirth. In the *Abhidhamma* a type of consciousness with this func-tion is called *paṭisandhi-citta* or (re)birth consciousness. Nineteen types of consciousness can perform the role of rebirth, namely the two (rootless) investigating types of consciousness with neutral feeling, the eight resultant wholesome types of consciousness, and

the nine resultant sublime (five fine-material and four immaterial) types of consciousness.[1]

2. Basic current of existence, or life-continuum. The Pali term *bhavaṅga* literally means 'factor of existence' and refers to an indispensable fact of life. During the course of our life, from rebirth consciousness until death consciousness, an undercurrent of consciousness takes place. This is where the mind falls back in between the active sensory, physical, mental and emotional experiences. In the context of Western psychology it might be called a subconscious undercurrent. Particularly in dreamless sleep there is this basic undercurrent. But even during the day countless *bhavaṅga-citta*s take place, in between all the thoughts and stimuli. The same nineteen *citta*s involved in rebirth perform the function of *bhavaṅga*.

3. Adverting. At a certain moment a *citta* will arise from the types of consciousness that have the function of *bhavaṅga*, and that *citta* adverts to an object that is perceived at one of the five sense-doors or at the mind-door. This moment of adverting to an object is called *āvajjana* and it is performed by two *citta*s, namely the first and the second functional rootless types of consciousness.

4–8. Seeing, hearing, smelling, tasting and touching. These five functions and the *citta*s that perform these tasks are conditioned by the nature of the object that presents itself. If form or colour appears then eye-consciousness arises, if there is a sound then ear-consciousness arises, and so on. It concerns very rudimentary

---

1   There are no unwholesome resultant types of consciousness (with unwholesome roots) because in that case there would be no rebirth as a human being but as an animal, hungry ghost, jealous demi-god or as a being in an invisible hell realm. See chapter 6.

sensory moments of consciousness of merely seeing, hearing, smelling, tasting or touching. Ten rootless *cittas* perform these functions, namely the first five that arise as the result of unwholesome *kamma*, and the first five that arise as the result of (slightly) wholesome *kamma*. Five pairs are always involved: two types of consciousness concerning visual objects, two concerning audible objects, two for smell, two for taste and two for touch.

Table 15.1: Functions

Explanation: The figures in the circles refer to the number of functions the respective types of consciousness can perform.

–   Twelve unwholesome

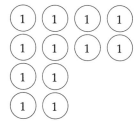

–   Eighteen rootless

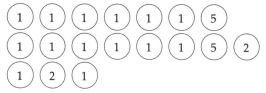

– Twenty-four wholesome

– Twenty-seven sublime

– Forty supramundane

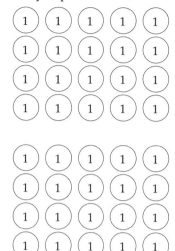

9–11. Receiving, investigating and determining. These functions have already been illustrated by the model for cognitive processes (table 3.1 in chapter 3). After sense consciousness has taken place the object—for example, the colour or the sound—is first of all received more clearly (*sampaṭicchana*). Subsequently it is investigated, not in an intellectual way but directly (*santīrana*): what is happening? Then a moment of determining arises (*votthapana*): is it wholesome or unwholesome?[2] The two rootless receiving types of consciousness have the function of receiving, the three rootless investigating types of consciousness have the function of investigating, and the mind-door adverting consciousness has the function of determining. All these types of consciousness can be found among the rootless *citta*s mentioned in chapter 3.

---

2   If it concerns a mental object, the determining *citta* arises immediately after a few *bhavaṅga-citta*s; the object is not first received and investigated.

12. Mental scanning. The Pali term *javana* is difficult to translate. It literally means 'quickly going over an object' or 'running through the object', and it is often translated as 'mental impulse'. It refers to types of consciousness that colour the object mentally or emotionally with anger, kindness and so on. In this phase the wholesome or unwholesome *cittas* arise; these give the object an emotional aspect. Eighty-seven *cittas* can take on the function of *javana*, namely the twelve unwholesome types of consciousness, the smile-producing-consciousness, the eight active wholesome and the eight functional wholesome types of consciousness, the nine active and the nine functional sublime types of consciousness, and the forty supramundane types of consciousness.

13. Registration. This is the function of a type of consciousness that commits the object to memory after it is perceived by the mental scanning process of the *javana-cittas*. This only happens when an object has manifested itself quite prominently and therefore has made an impression. Registration takes place with the three (rootless) investigating types of consciousness or with the eight resultant wholesome types of consciousness.

14. Death. Just as only one rebirth consciousness arises, we also experience only one death consciousness. This moment is called *cuti-citta* and announces the end of an existence.[3] The same nineteen *cittas* that were mentioned in the first and the second functions (conception and *bhavanga*) can take on the function of death consciousness.

---

3   See table 4.1 in chapter 4.

ASSIGNMENT

· ·

Table 15.1 illustrates all of the types of consciousness; it shows how many functions a type of consciousness can perform.
–   Question 1: Which *cittas* can have five functions? And what are these functions?[4]
–   Question 2: Which *cittas* can have four functions? And what are these functions?[5]
–   Question 3: Which *cittas* can have three functions? And what are these functions?[6]
–   Question 4: Which *cittas* can have two functions? And what are these functions?[7]
–   Question 5: Which *cittas* can have one function? And what is this function?[8]

---

4   Answer to question 1: The two neutral investigating types of consciousness can perform five functions, namely those of rebirth consciousness, *bhavaṅga*, death consciousness, registration and investigation.

5   Answer to question 2: The eight wholesome resultant types of consciousness can perform four functions, namely those of rebirth consciousness, *bhavaṅga*, death consciousness and registration.

6   Answer to question 3: The nine sublime resultant types of consciousness can perform three functions, namely those of rebirth consciousness, *bhavaṅga* and death consciousness.

7   Answer to question 4: The investigating type of consciousness with joy, and the mind-door adverting consciousness can perform two functions. The investigating type of consciousness accompanied by joy performs the functions of investigating and registration; the mind-door adverting consciousness performs the functions of determination and of adverting.

8   Answer to question 5: All the remaining types of consciousness perform one function. Eighty-seven of these perform the function of scanning (*javana*), namely the twelve unwholesome, the smile-producing, the eight active wholesome, the nine active sublime, the nine functional sublime and the forty supramundane types of consciousness. The first five rootless types of consciousness of the first row, and the first five rootless types of consciousness of the second row—together these are also called the five pairs of sense-consciousness (*dvipañcaviññāna-cittas*)—perform the function of seeing, hearing, smelling, tasting or touching. The two receiving types of consciousness perform only the function of receiving. The type

Doors

The term 'door' (*dvāra* in Pali) is a metaphor that is used in the *Abhidhamma* to indicate the means of communication between consciousness and the internal and external world. Six sense-doors are distinguished, namely the five senses (eyes, ears, nose, tongue and body) and the mind-door.

The five sense-doors

Through the eye forty-six *citta*s take place, namely the (rootless) five sense-door adverting *citta*s, the two forms of eye-consciousness, the two receiving types of consciousness, the three investigating types of consciousness, the mind-door adverting *citta* in the determining function,[9] twenty-nine types of consciousness in the scanning function (*javana*)—the twelve unwholesome *citta*s, eight active and eight functional wholesome *citta*s and the smile-producing-consciousness—and finally eight of the eleven types of consciousness in the function of registration (*tadārammana*)—the eight resultant wholesome types of consciousness.[10] Through the ear, the nose, the tongue and the body forty-six types of consciousness can take place, just as with the eye. In that case the two types of eye-consciousness are replaced by two forms of ear-consciousness, nose-consciousness, tongue-consciousness and body-consciousness.

---

of consciousness that adverts to the five sense-doors only performs the function of adverting.

9   See the previous chapter, the eleventh function.

10   The other three types of consciousness with the function of registration are the three investigating types of consciousness; these have already been mentioned. See chapter 1 for an explanation of cognitive processes.

The mind-door

Through the mind-door all mental processes (see table 3.2 in chapter 3) take place. Ninety-nine *citta*s can take place through the mind-door and are not involved in the thinking process. Twenty-two types of consciousness do not take place through the mind-door, namely the five types of sense-door adverting consciousness, the five pairs of sense consciousness, the two receiving types of consciousness and the nine resultant sublime types of consciousness.

'Door-freed' cittas

Nineteen *citta*s can arise without doors. These are the *citta*s in the function of rebirth, *bhavaṅga* and death, namely the two (rootless) investigating types of consciousness with neutral feeling, the eight resultant wholesome types of consciousness, and the five resultant fine-material and the four resultant immaterial types of consciousness. The *citta*s in these functions do not take place through the sense-doors. They do not receive a new object but take only one of the three possible objects of the *javana*s in the dying process of the preceding existence (see chapter 4, the dying process), similar to the echo of a sound that happened in the past. According to the *Abhidhamma*, one of the three possible objects of the *javana*s in the dying process during the present life is taken as the object of the rebirth, *bhavaṅga* and death consciousness in the existence that follows immediately.

Table 15.2: Doors

Explanation: The types of consciousness with the number 0 are door-freed. The types of consciousness with the number 1 can take place through one door. The types of consciousness with the number 5 can take place through five doors, namely the eyes, the ears, the nose, the tongue and the body. The types of consciousness with the number 6 can take place through six doors, namely through the five sense-doors and through the mind-door. The types of consciousness with the numbers 0 and 6 (6/0) can be door-freed or take place through six doors.

– Twelve unwholesome

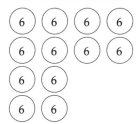

– Eighteen rootless

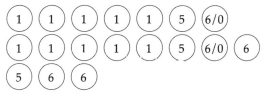

– Twenty-four wholesome

– Twenty-seven sublime

– Forty supramundane

(1)	(1)	(1)	(1)	(1)
(1)	(1)	(1)	(1)	(1)
(1)	(1)	(1)	(1)	(1)
(1)	(1)	(1)	(1)	(1)

(1)	(1)	(1)	(1)	(1)
(1)	(1)	(1)	(1)	(1)
(1)	(1)	(1)	(1)	(1)
(1)	(1)	(1)	(1)	(1)

THE BODY AND THE EXPERIENCE OF ENLIGHTENMENT

The previous parts of this book described the first two ultimate realities, namely consciousness and the mental factors. Chapter 16 of this part will discuss the third ultimate reality, namely matter or—applied to our lives as human beings— aspects of our physical existence. Chapter 17 introduces the connections of cause and effect between the first three ultimate realities, namely between consciousness, the mental factors and the body, and they are discussed by way of the model of dependent origination. Chapter 18 is devoted to the fourth ultimate reality: enlightenment. Chapter 19 discusses the relevance of the *Abhidhamma* in our everyday lives, especially for those of us who live in the West.

16

PHYSICAL LIFE

The previous parts of this book mainly dealt with our psyche. Besides a detailed description of our mental world, the *Abhidhamma* also gives an analysis of physical life. In this context the Pali term *rūpa* is used, which literally means 'that which is subject to change and decay'. This refers to the impermanent aspect of life. The term *rūpa* is often translated as 'matter' or as 'form'. Because we usually identify strongly with and get attached to the body, this translation offers an almost scientific objectivity. At times I have substituted the term 'matter' with words like 'physicality' or 'physical life', because the various forms of matter that are described below are specifically concerned with our body.

Twenty-eight types of matter

The *Abhidhamma* mentions twenty-eight aspects of the body, and of matter in general. *Rūpa* itself does not know, but it can be known or perceived with consciousness and its mental factors. Material phenomena arise and pass away somewhat slower than consciousness and its concomitants. In one moment of matter there are seventeen moments of consciousness. The twenty-eight forms of matter or material phenomena can be divided into eleven categories:

–   Four basic elements

◯◯◯◯

–   Five sense organs

◯◯◯◯◯

–   Four sense fields

◯◯◯◯

–   Two material phenomena of gender

◯◯

–   One heart-base

◯

–   One vitality

◯

–   One nutriment

◯

–   One space

◯

–   Two communication or expression

◯◯

–   Three changeability

◯◯◯

–   Four stages of material phenomena

◯◯◯◯

1–4. The four basic elements (dhātus)

The four basic elements of earth, fire, air and water are part of all forms of matter. Often one element is predominant, but all four are present and cannot be separated.

The earth element (*paṭhavīdhātu*) is the foundation for the other three basic elements, and it represents the principle of extension. It is experienced through touch, and in the meditation process as hardness or softness.

The fire element (*tejodhātu*) has the characteristic of heat, and its function is to mature or ripen material phenomena. It is experienced as heat or cold.

The air element (*vāyodhātu*) is responsible for motion and pressure. It transports matter to other places, and it has the characteristic of distension. It is experienced as tangible pressure, as movement and as heaviness or lightness.

The water element (*āpodhātu*) is mainly of abstract significance. It would seem obvious that the water element indicates the fluidity of phenomena, but this is not the case. According to the *Abhidhamma* we cannot experience fluidity. When we touch water we experience heat, cold, pressure, hardness or softness. Therefore the water element has a more abstract role, namely that of cohesion. It makes different particles of matter cohere, just as liquid turns dry ingredients into dough.

The four basic elements can be found in all matter. The other twenty-four forms of matter are all derived from these primary elements, which are also called 'the four essentials'.

5–9. The five sense organs (pasādarūpa)

The five sense organs refer to the subtle physical sensory systems or sensitive material phenomena that are located in the sense organs and with which we can see, hear, smell, taste and touch.

The eye-sensor, or the sensitive substance, is located in the retina and registers light, colour and form. The ear sensor is located in the ear cavity and registers sound. The nose sensor is located at the back of the nasal orifice and registers smell. The taste sensor is located in the taste buds on the tongue and registers taste. The touch sensor is the grossest of the sensors and is located in the skin. It serves to register touch and physical contact. The ears and the eyes are the subtlest of the sense organs. Seeing and hearing involves a very subtle 'tele-contact', because the colours or forms and the sounds come from a distance. If this was not so our eyes and ears could easily be damaged and we would become blind or deaf. With the nose, the tongue and the body there is direct contact: the smell, the taste and the touch take place directly on or in the respective sense organ.[1]

10–13. The four sense fields (gocararūpa)

The four sense fields include the material phenomena that can be perceived through the five senses. These are colour and form, sound vibrations, smell and taste. Touch is not perceived because one of the other sense fields is always predominant (for example cold, heat or hardness). Therefore four instead of five sense fields are mentioned.

14, 15. The two material phenomena of gender (bhāvarūpa)

The two forms of matter that are involved in gender manifest as masculinity and femininity. They are expressed, for instance, in the build of the body, in the hormones, and in the masculine or

---

1 The eyes and the ears are also considered as more refined because with them we can perceive people who have realised deep insights in their meditation process and who can listen to the Dhamma.

feminine way of moving. One might say this can be compared with the current theory of X and Y chromosomes.

16. The heart-base (hadayarūpa)

Heart-base refers to the material seat or support of consciousness and its concomitants. In the Buddhist world there has been a lot of discussion about where exactly consciousness is based: in the heart or in the brain. During the time of the Buddha the prevalent theory was that the heart was the seat of consciousness, but the Buddha very wisely did not make any definite statement in this regard. In this context he once said of consciousness that it was 'dependent on that material thing', without being explicit. In most commentaries, however, it was the heart that came to be viewed as the base for consciousness. Nowadays most Asian people point to their heart when they talk about the mind, whereas in the West people tend to point to the brain.

17. Vitality (jīvitindriya)

This is the physical variant of mental vitality, the sixth universal cetasika mentioned in chapter 8. Vitality ensures the presence and maintenance of matter. When we have used a lot of physical energy and feel tired, this form of physicality is not very prominent. As we get older the level of vitality gradually goes down, and it is completely extinguished when we die.

18. Nutriment (kabaḷīkārāhāra)

This form of matter does not refer to a bag of crisps but rather to the nutritional substance that can be found in edible food. These are the nutrients that nowadays are distinguished as vitamins, minerals, protein, carbohydrates and so on.

19. Space (ākāsadhātu)

According to the *Abhidhamma* the space element is the empty space between objects or matter. Space delineates the various material compounds and displays the boundaries of matter.

20, 21. Physical and verbal expression (viññattirūpa)

Analytically speaking, in expression physical processes take place. Both forms of expression are a direct result of types of consciousness. We communicate with physical and verbal expression and we convey our meanings and needs.

22–24. Changeability (vikārarūpa)

All material phenomena are subject to change. Three changing aspects are distinguished, namely lightness, malleability and wieldiness. Material or physical lightness (*lahutā*) dispels heaviness and is the opposite of dullness and sluggishness. It manifests as easy transformability. Material malleability (*mudutā*) has the characteristic of non-rigidity and softness; it manifests as the flexibility and malleability of matter. Wieldiness (*kammaññatā*) of matter dispels unwieldiness and is manifested as strength.

25–28. Four stages of material phenomena (lakkhaṇarūpa)

The last category includes the four stages of material or physical phenomena:

–   The arising or production of matter, or the physical aspect at conception

- The continuity and growth of matter or of the body, as can
  be observed in young people, or in flowers in spring or
  summer
- Decay or aging
- The disappearing or breaking up of matter. The arising,
  being present and falling away of material or physical
  phenomena is, according to the *Abhidhamma*, slower than
  the appearing, being present and disappearing of mental
  phenomena

Four causes for the arising of matter

According to the *Abhidhamma* there are four different causes for
the arising of material phenomena and physical processes, but
they are not mutually exclusive:

1. The law of cause and effect (*kamma*). This law of cause and
    effect creates our life, according to the Buddha's teachings.
    The twelve unwholesome types of consciousness and the
    five fine-material types of consciousness in a previous life
    can generate the physical existence in this life; these types of
    consciousness create physical processes.

2. Types of consciousness (*citta*). Consciousness in this life too
    generates physical processes. For example, consciousness
    with shame can cause us to blush, or when we are in love
    consciousness with sense desire can cause our hormones
    to go haywire. In fact, physical processes are already there
    from the very first *bhavaṅga-citta* in our life, and one hun-
    dred and seven of the one hundred and twenty-one types
    of consciousness can create matter. Only the ten rootless
    sense *citta*s and the four resultant immaterial types of

consciousness do not create matter.[2] The first two causes are mental, while the next two causes are physical.

3. Temperature (*utu*). Heat, cold and climate factors cause physical processes. When there is heat, for instance, we begin to sweat, while cold causes stagnation of the blood flow.

4. Nutrients (*āhāra*). This last factor causes plants, people and animals to grow, and in that sense it is an important cause for the origination of matter and for growth of the body.

EXCURSION: Illness

In previous generations, Western doctors paid relatively little attention to possible psychological causes of physical complaints. As a reaction, in the nineteen-seventies there was the tendency to 'psychologise' illness. Both approaches, however, can be detrimental.

When on the one hand the possible *psychological* aspects are not taken into account, a doctor may not be able to find obvious physical causes of an illness. Often the symptoms are no longer taken seriously, or are allayed by means of painkillers and the like.

When on the other hand the *physical* side is not taken into the equation, the cause of a complaint or an illness is sought in the psyche. In that case the somatic part is not checked properly, while from a bodily point of view there may be all kinds of problems. I have met many people who were victims of these two

---

2   The ten types of sense-consciousness are too weak, while the four immaterial resultant types of consciousness are not able to create matter because they take place in the immaterial sphere of consciousness.

limited approaches. It seems most sensible to me that in the case of persistent complaints both physical and mental causes should be investigated.

In the *Abhidhamma* texts all forms of matter and their causes are described in great detail. In this book, however, I will just offer a brief outline. Western science has, over the past few centuries, conducted extensive and detailed research into the nature and functioning of matter, so there is actually a lot of knowledge about this already. But in the West we have only just begun to study the mind, and in my view we could gain much insight from the detailed classifications and descriptions the *Abhidhamma* offers. This is also why in this book I have given more attention to how the mind works.

17

THE MODEL OF DEPENDENT ORIGINATION

So far we have discussed the three ultimate realities of existence, namely consciousness, the mental factors and the body. This chapter will show the connection between these realities by referring to the model of dependent origination (*paṭiccasamuppāda*). It shows a process of twelve links that are related to each other through cause and effect; it is a cycle that is controlled by ignorance, and it illustrates how we are thrown from one experience to the next, and how we suffer. The law of dependent origination and its twelve links is described in two ways, namely in the usual traditional way, and subsequently in a free, more psychological way. In the traditional explanation it concerns three periods: past lives, the present existence, and future lives. In the psychological approach only our experiences in the present existence are relevant. I would like to start with the traditional description.

1. Ignorance

In the twelve links of dependent origination there is in fact no real beginning or end. When the Buddha was asked whether there was a starting point somewhere he answered, after some deliberation, that if he were to indicate a beginningless beginning of suffering he would point to ignorance or lack of awareness (*avijjā*). In Buddhist psychology ignorance or unawareness is defined as not understanding, or misunderstanding, the Four Noble Truths. In illustrations of dependent origination, this first link is usually depicted as a blind person. The blind person cannot see where he walks; he lives in darkness. In the same way we are blinded by ignorance, and often we do not fully know what is happening in the here and now. In some sense we live in darkness. In the dark we cannot distinguish between what is the right way and what is not. We panic or get confused; we fall or hit our head over and over again. In this way we unconsciously create our own suffering.

The first link in dependent origination refers to *moha*, the fourteenth mental factor (see chapter 9). Through unawareness we continue to face problems. As shown in the previous chapter, according to Buddhist philosophy not *all* problems are the result of ignorance. We may fall ill due to organic causes, climate factors or food. But psychologically speaking ignorance plays such an important role that it is called the root cause of suffering. Through ignorance we have no freedom to choose the way in which we deal with the vicissitudes of life. Therefore we keep being imprisoned by habitual thought patterns ('I can't do this'), emotional patterns (depression, anxieties) and unwholesome behaviour patterns (addictions, abusing ourselves).

2. Kammic formations or volitions

With ignorance as the driving force we carry out volitional activities, *sankhāra* in Pali. This second link is symbolised by a potter making all kinds of pots and vases. Some are beautiful and others are failures; some are finished and others are still being made. In the same manner we physically, verbally and mentally carry out activities that lead to more harmony, but we also act in ways that cause damage and pain to ourselves and others. According to Buddhist psychology, a subtle form of unconsciousness accompanies most of the activities that we carry out, including wholesome acts like cultivating friendliness or practising generosity. Without being aware of it we are, for example, praising ourselves ('Look how well I am doing') or bargaining ('If I give this, then surely I will get something back'). Therefore most of our wholesome acts are also part of the cycle of dependent origination. The *Abhidhamma* considers twenty-nine types of consciousness as potential *kammic* formations, namely the twelve unwholesome, the eight active wholesome, the five active fine-material and the four active immaterial types of consciousness.

3. Rebirth consciousness

According to the traditional explanation of the law of dependent origination the first two links operate in the past: in previous lives or in different realms of existence or spheres of consciousness, as described in chapter 6. The third link, called *viññāṇa* or *paṭisandhi-citta*, refers to the moment of conception: the very first beginning of the present life. According to Buddhism, new life consciousness starts the moment a sperm cell gets into contact with an egg cell and rebirth consciousness is present. Thirty-two types of consciousness can function as rebirth consciousness, namely the first fifteen rootless types of consciousness, the eight resultant wholesome types of consciousness, and the nine resultant sublime *cittas*.

4. Body and mind

Although the *Abhidhamma* gives a very detailed description of all possible spheres of consciousness, in the chain of conditioned relations only the human existence is further analysed. From the moment of conception the human embryo starts to grow, and physical and mental development takes place. The fourth link is called *nāma-rūpa* in Pali. The oarsman in the drawing symbolises *nāma* and refers to all mental factors that arise with rebirth consciousness. The boat symbolises *rūpa* and implies all rudimentary physical phenomena produced by *kamma* and originating at conception.

5. The six senses

Following on from the fourth link the six human senses—the eyes, the ears, the nose, the tongue, the body and the mind—come  into being. With these six senses (*saḷāyatana*) we can see, hear, smell, taste, touch and think; they are depicted as a house with six doors. The first five senses are the five sense organs discussed in the previous chapter. The sixth sense refers to the thirty-two types of consciousness that were already mentioned at rebirth consciousness.[1]

---

1   See chapter 15 for more explanation of the six sense-doors.

6. Contact

In this life the six senses are constantly stimu-
lated. There are always moments of contact
between the senses, sense objects and sense
consciousness. For example, when a sound
comes together with the ear and a moment
of ear-consciousness, hearing takes place.
When the ear is not there, when there is no sound,
or when there is no cognitive perception by ear-consciousness, hearing does not take place. The same can be said
in relation to the other five senses. Sense impression means the
very first universal mental factor, *phassa*. This link is usually
represented by a kiss. The reason for this is possibly because a
kiss—particularly in Asia, where people don't kiss very much—is
an event that makes a deep impression. Whether we want to or
not, all these processes constantly take place, twenty-four hours
a day, and for the greater part of the day we are not aware or only
vaguely aware of them.

7. Feeling

Contact is always accompanied by feeling. This
sensory 'consumption', which is called *vedanā*,
is the second universal mental factor
discussed in chapter 8. Feeling can—as
shown in chapter 14—take five forms.
The sensory stimulus can physically and mentally
feel pleasant or unpleasant, and mentally it can also
be experienced as neutral. Because feeling has a strong influence
on our way of being and can be a strong catalyst for inner reactive

patterns, it is symbolised by a man with an arrow in his eye. As will become clear from the next links, feeling can totally blind us.

8. Desire

Feeling is a mental factor that simply arises whether we want it to or not. After the seventh link, however, we actually have a moment of choice in how we deal with the sensory stimulus and the accompanying feeling. In the model of dependent origination ignorance or unawareness is always present, like a general behind the scenes. Because of this unawareness we react in unskilful ways to the previous links. In fact, at the eighth link three different reactions should be described: namely the reaction to pleasant feeling, the reaction to unpleasant feelings, and the reaction to neutral feelings. In the model for dependent co-arising the Buddha probably chose pleasant feelings as the point of departure because desire—to survive, to procreate, and so on—is much more fundamental in nature. As human beings we are continually looking for pleasant feelings, and we are driven by desire, or *taṇhā*, a term that can also be translated as hankering, pining, craving, thirst, lust or grasping.

Desire or greed is depicted as an elephant with an unquenchable thirst drinking gin. If we were experiencing an unpleasant feeling at the seventh link, the picture might be imagined as a fighting man. He experiences desire 'in the opposite direction', namely the desire not to have a certain thing or experience. When the feeling is neutral we could imagine someone watching television without any interest or staring ahead apathetically. Desire is the eighteenth (unwholesome) mental factor mentioned in chapter 9.

9. Attachment

Desire that is unconsciously followed leads to attachment, grasping or clinging to the object onto which the desire is projected. According to Buddhist psychology, attachment or *upādāna* is the tendency to maintain desire and to get it satisfied again and again. This tendency is usually drawn as a monkey in a tree, which refers to two traditional Asian ways of catching monkeys.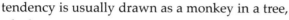

The first way is where the monkey catcher hollows out a coconut and makes a hole in the shell that is just big enough for the monkey's hand to fit through. The monkey catcher hangs this coconut close to a suitable bait (for example, a bunch of bananas) in such a way that the monkey can get to the bananas only if it puts its hand through the hole in the coconut. The monkey catcher hides and waits. The monkey sees the bunch of bananas, puts its hand through the hole in the coconut, and catches hold of a banana. It wants to get the banana to its mouth but realises that the banana does not fit through the hole in the coconut. Instead of letting go of the banana, the monkey starts to scream loudly and keeps trying to pull its hand back through the hole while still holding the banana, even though this is impossible. Because it is attached to its desire, the monkey is now an easy prey for the monkey catcher.

Another way of catching monkeys is to suspend a bunch of bananas over a tree trunk covered with glue. The monkey, wanting to get to the bananas, first notices its front paw sticking to the glue and tries to release it by using its other paw. The other front paw also gets stuck; subsequently its hind paws and eventually its whole body is stuck. These two stories illustrate the sticky nature of attachment.

As humans we all experience one or more forms of attachment, and often we are even attached to our attachments. Four forms of attachment are distinguished:

1. Attachment to sensory stimuli. We easily get attached to what we see, hear, smell, taste and touch. In this way, for example, we cannot take our eyes off a beautiful man or woman. In some cases we feel unhappy without an iPod or having the radio on in the car. We buy expensive perfumes and we have high expectations of food. This deeply rooted search for sensory pleasures is also expressed in addictions to cigarettes, coffee, alcohol, sedatives, drugs, sex, gambling, computer games, watching television or surfing the Internet.

2. Attachment to ideas, theories and thought patterns. We can also identify strongly with, for example, a political or religious worldview. Or to a psychological self image or an image of mankind: 'I am unworthy' or 'Nobody can be trusted'.

3. Attachment to rites and rituals. This refers to religious or non-religious activities that are carried out automatically and without mindfulness. Examples of this are being convinced that we can be happy only when we drink the water from a certain river or that we can prevent harm by sacrificing an animal. And, perhaps more recognisably, the habitual patterns we all use to give structure to our lives. We may always start the day with porridge or with toast and jam. Or we always carry out a ritual to double check whether we locked the door when we leave the house. Such patterns can sometimes become pathological, as is the case with people who suffer from extreme forms of compulsive or obsessive disorders.

4. Attachment to the idea that there is a 'self' or a soul. The last form of attachment mentioned is related to the idea that there is a soul or a 'self' in the form of a solid, unchangeable, eternal substance or essence within ourselves or outside ourselves (Allah, God). In this respect Buddhism has a very unique view of the world, namely that in the ultimate sense there is no everlasting soul; that there is no unchanging 'self', and no higher entity that controls or regulates life. Even though we create the idea of a 'self', a soul or a higher entity, according to Buddhist psychology life is in fact nothing but the continuous arising and passing away of physical, sensory, cognitive and emotional processes, subject to change and without a solid entity in or behind it. The *Visuddhimagga* says that, 'In the ultimate sense there is no doer who does the deed, nor can anyone be found who consumes the fruit. Only mental and physical processes continually arise and pass away'.

The first form of attachment is a reinforced type of desire, while the other three forms of attachment are expressed as a combination of desire and wrong view (*diṭṭhi*), the nineteenth mental factor that was described in chapter 9.

10. Becoming

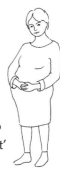

Attachment leads to emotional reactions and new thought patterns that are aimed at maintaining what we are attached to. When, for instance, we are attached to smoking and the packet of cigarettes is nearly finished, we get anxious and make plans to buy a new packet. In those moments we are 'pregnant' with a new action. Examples of emotional patterns resulting from attachment are conceit, anger, sadness, fear and insecurity. We respond to this immediately by making new plans to satisfy the attachment.

In the Buddhist teachings two types of becoming are distinguished, namely *kammabhava* and *upapattibhava*. *Kammabhava* refers to the active behavioural patterns in speech, action and thought; these are controlled by the twenty-nine active types of consciousness that were mentioned in the second link. *Upapattibhava* refers to the thirty-two resultant types of consciousness in the third link of dependent origination; these are the result of active behavioural patterns. Both are based on attachment. They are usually depicted as a pregnant woman, and together they form the link of becoming (*bhava* in Pali). The second link in dependent co-arising—volitional activities—refers to the past, *kammabhava* is happening in the present, and *upapattibhava* takes place in the future sphere of consciousness. Becoming represents the unconscious mental driving forces and the rebirth consciousness that in turn leads to the next link.

11. (Re)birth

From the tenth link a new conception and a new birth arise. This birth, or *jāti*, takes place in one of the six realms described in chapter 6. All possible types of consciousness, mental factors and physical processes that are part of a new life are represented in this link.

12. Old age and death

Birth is the beginning of a new life, which is subject again to old age (*jarā*) and death (*marana*),
and to all possible forms of suffering that are
part and parcel of human existence. In many
Buddhist monasteries these forms of suffering are
recited daily in Pali. The recitation goes like this:

> Birth is suffering; old age is suffering; death is suf-
> fering; sorrow, lamentation, pain, dissatisfaction and
> despair are suffering; being confronted with what is
> undesirable gives rise to pain and conflict; loosing
> what we desire or love gives rise to suffering; not being
> able to obtain what we desire gives rise to suffering.
> In brief: the five aspects of human existence, which
> we make our own and to which we are attached, are
> suffering. Body, feelings, perception, conditioning and
> sensory consciousness are a source of stress, frustra-
> tion and suffering.

The chain of dependent origination is a process of cause and effect
that we are only partly or not at all aware of. The Buddha taught
that only awareness or mindfulness can break this chain. If we
continue to live unconsciously we remain imprisoned, shackled
to patterns of thought and behaviour that become stronger all
the time. And if ignorance is maintained this driving force will
probably keep growing, which means that we return to the first
link and continue to suffer.

Further analysis: three periods

The model of dependent arising described above is further explained in the *Abhidhamma* in various ways. This model covers three periods: namely previous lives, the present life, and future lives. According to the traditional explanation the first two links (ignorance and volitions) take place in previous lives. The next eight links (rebirth consciousness, body and mind, the six senses, contact, feeling, desire, attachment and becoming) take place in the present existence. The last two links (rebirth, old age and death) take place in a future existence.

Cause and effect

Another perspective is that with regard to cause and effect. Here the model is divided into four groups:

1. Causes in the past: ignorance (1) and volitional activities in the past (2) have caused our present existence and our present behavioural and thought patterns.

2. Effects in the present existence: rebirth consciousness (3), body and mind (4), the six senses (5), contact (6) and feeling (7) arose as a natural consequence of causes in the past, just as a plant grows from a seed.

3. Causes in the present existence: according to the Buddha's teachings we cause new patterns in this life through desire (8), attachment (9) and becoming (10), for in the present moment we let ourselves be swept along by desire, attachment and our plans for the future.

4. Effects in the future: the last two links of dependent arising—(re)birth (11), and old age and death (12)—are the natural results of driving forces in the present existence.

Three rounds

Another way of looking at the chain of dependent arising is with regard to the three so-called rounds (*vatta* in Pali):

1. The round of defilements. Ignorance, desire and attachment are considered the three driving forces that are the basis for the whole model. They are obstacles to the realisation of profound happiness, and they are the root causes of the suffering we experience.

2. The round of actions, or the creation of *kamma*. Volitional activities in the past (link number 2) and becoming (link number 10, and in particular *kammabhava*, or the active behavioural patterns in speech, actions and thoughts that we show in this life) are part of this second round.

3. The round of results, or *vipāka*. This last round includes all other links, namely rebirth consciousness, body and mind, the six senses, contact, feeling, becoming, and then in particular that which refers to the future sphere of consciousness and which is called *upapattibhava*, (re)birth, old age and death.

The three divisions have been illustrated as follows:

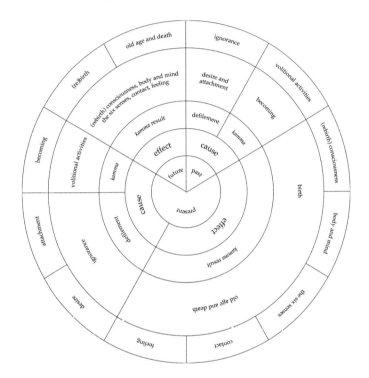

The psychological explanation of the law of dependent origination

If we do not believe in the concept of previous and future lives the *paṭiccasamuppāda* can easily become an abstract theory that we do not know how to apply. But the Buddha clearly stated that his teachings are to be tested directly, here and now, without having to believe blindly in something we cannot see or recognise. So if you do not believe in past or future lives there is also a practical explanation of the chain of dependent co-arising that came about later. The complete model can also be recognised only when we apply it to this life. This psychological approach briefly looks like this:

With unconsciousness as the driving force (1) we have established all kinds of conditionings in this life (2). These conditioned patterns have resulted in birth in the present moment (3) with the current characteristics of body and mind (4). Through the senses (5) we experience all kinds of sensory stimuli (6). These impressions are accompanied by feelings (7). Because of unawareness we automatically respond to them with desire, aversion and other emotional reactions, and we attach to or identify with what we experience (9). In order to maintain these forms of attachment we develop all kinds of new inner patterns, first of all in our thinking (10) and subsequently also in our actions (11). These new actions are starting a life of their own again, resulting in new or stronger forms of suffering (12). In turn, we can't cope well with these new or more persistent forms of stress and tension, which means that unawareness increases and we end up again at the first link. In this way we remain entangled in a vicious circle.

To make this model more specific, I will give a practical example of how dependent origination works.

Joan learns from childhood on that she has to do her best and that she should always be ready to help others. Unconsciously she internalises this message (1). After secondary school she works for some time in a geriatric nursing home (2). The workload there is quite heavy. Because she feels that she can not help people in satisfactory ways, she starts to look for a new job and eventually finds one (3). She begins work in the service sector and every day she talks to people who have problems. Joan likes her work and she feels that she is doing well in this new job (4).

Over the next year, due to innovations and to colleagues being on sick leave, her workload becomes heavier and there is more and more to do (5). She finds it increasingly difficult to deal with all the stimuli (6) due to these changes. She does not feel well about this (7). Joan begins to suffer from fatigue and strain, and strongly desires to get another job (8). Soon this desire begins to play a big part in her life (9) and she starts to make plans for the future (10). She starts to apply for jobs, and after some time she is fortunate enough to get another job (11). However, quite soon she discovers that in the new workplace there is talk of serious reshuffling, and there is a culture of complaining, which badly affects the atmosphere at work (12). And Joan realises too that she is not in fact fully recovered from the fatigue symptoms that arose in the previous job. But she ignores these signals (1) and begins to work even harder (2). And so on and so forth.

Transcending the negative spiral

The law of dependent origination can be described as a downward spiral that results in more and more stress and suffering caused by lack of awareness. In this sense it is an expression of the first two Noble Truths described in chapter 12.

Is it possible to liberate ourselves from this strangling spiral? According to the *Abhidhamma* it is! The Eightfold Path—the fourth Noble Truth, with mindfulness as its central factor—is a way out of this prison. When we become aware of feelings, desires, attachments or other links we transcend for that moment the chain of dependent origination. We experience the third Noble Truth: the cessation of suffering. When, for instance, we are aware of a pleasant feeling and we label it as such, then desire may still arise, but it no longer happens automatically. There is a subtle inner spaciousness so that desire no longer arises as a conditioned, automatic reaction.

We can compare this to an island dweller who usually can travel quite easily from one end of the island to the other. But if a cyclone breaks up the island and divides it into two smaller islands, the islander will find it less easy to travel to the other part of the island; it will take more time and effort. He will be more inclined to investigate the island he is on and try to find other food. In a similar way mindfulness creates a wedge or space in which conditioned reactions will happen less automatically. The mind can stay with just experiencing feeling, and more space may arise for different ways of living.

Mindfulness therefore gives inner space and offers us the possibility to realise the fourth ultimate reality: enlightenment.

18

THE EXPERIENCE OF ENLIGHTENMENT

Chapter 7 introduced the experience of enlightenment and the liberating effect of this. *Nibbāna*[1] is the fourth and last ultimate reality. It involves the cessation of or liberation from the entanglements we usually experience that are caused by desire, hatred and ignorance. In this way we can escape from the miserable cycle of dependent origination that was discussed in the previous chapter.

The threefold happiness of mindfulness

In every moment of mindfulness we can in fact already experience 'threefold happiness' and get a taste of enlightenment:

1. Being aware of what is clearly presenting itself in or to us already gives inner space. The flow of ignorance (*moha*) is temporarily put to a halt; we are aware of what is happening in our life in the moment, and we are not in darkness.

2. The second aspect of mindfulness that leads to happiness is included in the accepting attitude towards what is

---

1   In Sanskrit the term *nirvāna* is used, and this term has also been introduced into the English language. I decided, however, to use the Pali term *nibbāna* in this book, because that is what is used in the Abhidhamma texts of *Theravāda* Buddhism.

presenting itself. Acceptance or recognition is healing. We are allowed to be as we are, and we are not conditioned by aversion or hatred (*dosa*).

3. Acceptingly but also objectively noting or naming what is clearly presenting itself enables us to be aware of experiences without identifying with them. The subtle naming or noting gives us the space to observe without attachment (*lobha*) what is happening, as if we are watching these processes in somebody else.

For a few years now I have given participants a feedback form at the end of a retreat. The responses give me more insight into the organisational and practical aspects of retreats, and I also gain a better understanding of the effects of mindfulness practice. Anna sent me the following story, which illustrates the threefold happiness we can taste with the practice of mindfulness:

> The day after the retreat I was at a meeting of about one hundred and fifty people in a smallish space. This caused a panic attack—I have had these before in similar situations—and I got overwhelmed by it. I desperately tried to find a way out of this situation but could see no other solution than to leave the room, which would be difficult. Nor could I see how the meditation would help me, until I suddenly realised: 'This is unpleasant'. By becoming aware of it, to accept it and to note it mentally I noticed that I was no longer totally involved in the unpleasant feeling, I was no longer the victim of this feeling. And the fearful feelings just passed, and there were no after-effects either in the sense of: 'Here she goes again with her panic attacks' or 'What if it happens again next week'.

Mindfulness is the foundation for the happiness of liberating insight, and therefore a moment of mindfulness is called *khanika-vimutti*, or momentary liberation. At that moment we are not imprisoned or entangled in the clutches of desire, hatred and delusion. When by means of the practice of insight meditation we are mindful for a longer period of time we realise *vikkham-bhana-vimutti*, or long-term liberation. When mindfulness finally is fully developed we can realise enlightenment with the supra-mundane types of consciousness. This is called *samuccheda-vimutti*, or complete liberation, because the forces of desire, hatred and ignorance—the causes of suffering—are completely extinguished. When the *Abhidhamma* speaks of enlightenment it means this last form of liberation.

Complete peace

The *Abhidhamma* describes the the enlightenment experience as onefold, twofold or threefold.

Onefold: Complete or perfect peace

The nature of *nibbāna* is onefold and has the characteristic of complete or perfect peace (*santilakkhaṇa* in Pali). This peace is called complete because the experience of enlightenment is unrelated to all the usual sensory, mental and emotional processes, and it is not subject to change. In that sense *nibbāna* is also called uncon-ditioned (*asankhata*). It offers us absolute freedom.

Twofold: Enlightenment with and without residue

Enlightenment is twofold in the sense that it can be experienced in two ways, namely with and without residue. Someone who has realised the highest enlightenment and can therefore be called an *arahat* realises 'enlightenment with a residue' (*sa-upādisesa-nibbāna*).[2] Their mind is already completely purified, but they still experience residual fuel in the form of mental and physical impressions. An *arahat* therefore can experience physical pain but will not suffer mentally because of it. At death an *arahat* attains *anupādisesa-nibbāna*: all mental and physical experiences come to an end. Because there is no longer *kammic* force for a rebirth, this is called 'enlightenment without a residue': all suffering has now been completely eradicated. The difference between with or without residue is also described as (1) the extinguishing of destructive forces (defilements), and (2) the extinguishing of all aspects of human existence (the aggregates).

Threefold: Three extraordinary characteristics

Nibbāna is threefold in that it has three specific characteristics:

1. Spaciousness or emptiness (*suññattā*). The enlightenment experience is called empty because it is free from desire, hatred and ignorance, and because it is free from conditioning. Meditation teachers say that spaciousness or emptiness is experienced by meditators who in their practice, just before the enlightenment experience, are specifically aware of the uncontrollability and selfless nature of all phenomena.

2. Formlessness (*animitta*). Enlightenment does not have form or colour and cannot be described according to our usual frame of reference. Meditators who experience

---

2   See chapter 7 for details about the experience of enlightenment.

enlightenment in this way come in contact with the supra-mundane through a deep sense of impermanence.

3. Freedom from desire (*appaṇihita*). The experience of enlightenment is free from desire. Meditators realise *nibbāna* in this way through the gateway of pain and suffering.

The Buddha taught that our everyday experiences are impermanent and unsatisfactory; *nibbāna*, however, is permanent and blissful. Both our everyday experiences and the experience of enlightenment are considered to be without 'self'.

19

THE VALUE OF THE *ABHIDHAMMA* FOR CONTEMPORARY WESTERNERS

In this last chapter I would like to try to answer a very essential and practical question: 'What use is all this knowledge to us? What is the value of it for people who live in a completely different (Western) culture? Is it not sufficient just to meditate without all this intellectual baggage?'

As the scriptures show, it is not necessary to accumulate intellectual knowledge in order to be able to taste the many fruits of Buddhist practice. The Buddha gave many people only simple and immediately applicable advice, which enabled them to realise the highest stages of insight. Yet the study of the *Abhidhamma*—which literally means 'higher teachings'—is highly praised and encouraged by many Buddhists, and great numbers of monks, nuns and meditation teachers study the *Abhidhamma* teachings sooner or later during the course of their training. I would like to voice a number of valuable aspects of (the study of) the *Abhidhamma* below.

The intellectual foundation of spirituality

The *Abhidhamma* offers a clear and consistent foundation for the spiritual path: a theoretical frame of reference, or 'web of wisdom'. Soon after I had been introduced to insight meditation I went without hesitation on a long and intensive retreat. I did so from blind faith and hardly knew what I was letting myself in for. Only later did I get to know and understand the why and how of meditation, through reading books and talking with people. I often meet people who have a different approach, people who feel the need to have more information beforehand about the practice of meditation and its effects. Through *Abhidhamma* courses analytically minded people can be encouraged to start practising meditation, and they can do so in a much more informed way. In addition, combining scientific research into the effects of meditation with the detailed phenomenological descriptions in the *Abhidhamma* offers confidence and enables the healing and liberating teachings of the Buddha to become more widely known.[1]

A light on the path

The detailed map of our mind offers knowledge of and insight into the workings of our psyche. I noticed this when during *Abhidhamma* study I began to recognise all kinds of things in myself. For instance, I had never realised that sometimes I could be miserly or proud. By reading about it I could suddenly recognise this more clearly in myself, and this immediately created more space so that I was less consumed or controlled by these forces. Insight works as a light on a dark road—when we walk carefully and not too quickly we may be able to find our way in the dark, but lights along the way make walking a lot easier. The insightful structures of the *Abhidhamma* offer such a light.[2]

---

1   See for example the book *Destructive Emotions* by Daniel Goleman, the best-selling author of *Emotional Intelligence*.

2   It is good to point out that the *Abhidhamma* and the practice of insight meditation can have a positive influence on each other. The study of the *Abhidhamma* offers intellectual insights, while the practice of *vipassanā* results in intuitive insights.

Getting acquainted with other psychological frameworks

Becoming familiar with other perspectives on life and with other worldviews can enrich us. A few years ago, in conversation with my Burmese meditation teacher, Sayadaw U Kundalabhivamsa, I came upon a noticeable difference between Eastern and Western ideas or views. When some time into a long retreat I could hardly see any progress in my meditation practice, I started to complain to him about this. I had been doing whatever I could in the practice, but nothing was happening. I wondered whether defects in my upbringing could be the cause for the fact that the meditation process was—in my view—progressing far too slowly. Did I perhaps not receive enough love from my parents? Had I not learned to be kind and mild enough towards myself? I was confused. Talking with me in private, my teacher offered a completely different option. He mentioned four types of meditators:

1. Meditators who without difficulty and very quickly are able to reap the fruits of the meditative path; according to my teacher this was because these meditators had been practising *samatha* and *vipassanā* meditation in a previous life.

2. Meditators who very quickly but with great difficulty (pain) make progress in their practice; this was the case because in a previous life they had practised *vipassanā* but not *samatha*.

3. Meditators who without difficulty but slowly come to the core of the practice; these meditators had practised *samatha* in previous lives, but not *vipassanā*.

4. Meditators who slowly and with great difficulty reap the fruits of the meditative path; in previous lives they had practised neither *samatha* nor *vipassanā*.

It was immediately clear to me in which category I belonged. Apart from this it was also very liberating to view my life from a completely different angle, and my complaints quickly melted away.

Insight into the identification mechanism

The last, and in my view the most important, function of the *Abhidhamma* is to get what I would call 'insight into the identification mechanism'. Usually we are not that aware of what is happening here and now. As a result we have from a young age onwards developed a distorted image of reality. Through unawareness and careless observation we have, and we cultivate, the tendency to interpret or colour our experiences as 'self' or 'mine'. This identification is usually quite strong, and it is not only expressed in the subjective perception of external objects but also takes place with regard to the body, sense objects, thoughts, physical feelings and emotions. These phenomena and experiences then easily get (unconsciously) interpreted and claimed as '*my* body', '*my* thoughts', '*my* feelings' and so on.

Through identification with all these experiences we become afraid to lose them, and sadness arises when the experiences or objects we identified with disappear again. It also becomes much more difficult to deal with feelings of pain and discomfort, because we consider them a hostile attack on '*my* leg' or '*my* back'.

According to Buddhist psychology this identification mechanism is in fact a deeply rooted, veiled and mistaken view of reality. In fact there is no 'I' involved; there is only a series of consecutive moments in which types of consciousness manifest themselves and are accompanied by a number of mental factors. All these moments have a beginning and an end, and they are related as cause and effect. Conventionally speaking we can say 'I', 'you' or 'mine'—for example, 'I am writing a book' and 'you are reading this chapter'. In the ultimate sense, however, there are just physical and mental phenomena that arise and pass away again.[3]

The above may be compared to a football club, for example Manchester United. When we talk about Manchester United everybody knows what we mean: the well-known football club from England. When we analyse the club, however, it turns out that everything is in flux. The players of twenty years ago have gone, there is another coach and a new manager, and even the old stadium has completely changed. To make communication easier we talk about Manchester United, but in reality there is no solid substance to be found in the club.

The *Abhidhamma* offers an intellectual framework through which we can better understand the universal characteristic of 'no-self' (*anattā* in Pali). When practising insight meditation, we become at a profound level aware of 'no-self' by objectively noting thoughts, feelings and other meditation experiences, just as a scientist who is studying a phenomenon. Therefore we don't note physical discomfort as '*my* pain' but as 'pain', we don't label thoughts as '*my* thought' but as 'thinking', and so on. In this way the idea or concept of a 'self' becomes transparent and we develop an attitude of non-identification with what presents itself.

Inner flexibility

For some people the idea of 'no-self' seems rather threatening,

---

3   In the preface I gave the definition of psychology as 'the science that is concerned with the study of the phenomena of consciousness'. Another definition of psychology could be: 'the study of a person and his character'. It could be said that the *Abhidhamma* studies and analyses the concepts of 'person' and 'character' to such an extent that the whole notion of 'person' disintegrates and turns out to be based only on an idea we have, and does not exist as an ultimate reality.

and yet it offers a lot of inner space. Particularly in our Western culture we are inclined to feel very much responsible for what we experience, and this is a heavy mental burden. We feel guilty, perhaps, just because thoughts or emotions may arise that we consider unacceptable. We then blame ourselves for not living up to our self-image. A deeper understanding of 'no-self' leads to inner flexibility and big-heartedness. Of course this does not mean that we do not need to take responsibility for what arises in our consciousness. Precisely because we gain more insight into our lives, however, we can learn to deal more skilfully with the stimuli and situations we are faced with, and to approach them with wise attention. In this way we learn to live with more gentleness and kindness, and we don't need to get stuck into all the different judgements and limitations we place on ourselves (and on others). Furthermore, we no longer need to invest so much energy in forcefully trying to have everything our own way, which means that we can more easily flow with the natural current of life. This offers an inner freedom that can be compared to leaving behind superfluous luggage during a long trek.

EPILOGUE

With the description of enlightenment we have now examined all four ultimate realities. Part 1 and part 2 introduced consciousness, part 3 dealt with the mental factors, part 4 illustrated the associations between the types of consciousness and the mental factors, and part 5 described matter and the enlightenment experience. There are, however, a number of themes that I have either not dealt with or only briefly discussed here. A lot more could be said about matter, rebirth and the various cognitive processes, for instance, and we have not even considered the rather complex theory concerning the twenty-four conditions, or *paccayadhammā*. Even without that additional depth, though, I still believe that this book is a valuable introduction to the world of the *Abhidhamma*.

May *The Web of Buddhist Wisdom* lead to a better understanding of these subtle Buddhist teachings and bring about liberating insight into the impermanent, vulnerable and ultimately selfless nature of our existence.

BUDDHIST LISTS

As mentioned in chapter 1, in the Buddhist teachings there are lists for many different phenomena. These lists serve as a framework to help students or readers remember what they have learnt, and to transmit the basic elements of the teachings. This appendix will gather together a number of these lists, which are divided into four groups: lists of phenomena or factors that are general, that bring about suffering, that bring about happiness, and that lead to liberation.

General lists

The three universal characteristics (*tilakkhaṇa*):

1. Impermanence (*anicca*)
2. Unsatisfactoriness (*dukkha*)
3. Uncontrollability or 'no-self' (*anattā*)

The Four Noble Truths (*ariyasaccāni*):

1. There is suffering (*dukkha-sacca*)
2. There is a cause of suffering (*dukkhasamudaya-sacca*)
3. Cessation of suffering is possible (*dukkhanirodha-sacca*)
4. there is a path that leads to the cessation of suffering (*dukkhanirodha-gāminīpaṭipadā*)[1]

---

1   This refers to the Eightfold Path.

The four ultimate realities (*paramattha-dhammā*):

1. Consciousness (*citta*)
2. Mental factors that are associated with consciousness (*cetasikas*)
3. The body, or matter (*rūpa*)
4. The experience of enlightenment (*nibbāna*)

The four sources of nourishment for physical life (*ahāras*):

1. The law of cause and effect (*kamma*)
2. Consciousness (*citta*)
3. Climate factors and organic factors (*utu*)
4. Physical food (*kabaḷīkārāhāra*)

The five aggregates[2] (*pañcakkhandhā*):

1. The body (*rūpa*)
2. Feelings (*vedanā*)
3. Perception (*saññā*)
4. Volitional activities (*sankhāra*)
5. Consciousness (*viññāṇa*)

---

2 'Aggregates' or 'constituents' is the usual translation of this Pali term. What it refers to is the five aspects of a human being with which we easily identify and to which we are easily attached.

Lists of factors that are unwholesome and the causes of suffering

The four taints or influxes (*āsava*):[3]

1. Sensual desire (*kāmāsava*)
2. The desire to be or to become (*bhavāsava*)
3. Wrong views (*diṭṭhāsava*)
4. Ignorance or delusion (*avijjāsava*)

The four forms of attachment or clinging (*upādāna*):

1. Clinging to sensual pleasure (*kāmupādāna*)
2. Clinging to wrong views (*diṭṭhupādāna*)
3. Clinging to rites and rituals (*sīlabbatupādāna*)
4. Clinging to the notion that there is a self (*attavādupādāna*)

The five afflictive emotions or hindrances[4] (*nīvaraṇas*):

1. Sense desire (*kāmacchanda*)
2. Aversion (*byāpāda*)
3. Drowsiness and sluggishness (*thīna-middha*)
4. Restlessness and remorse (*uddhacca* and *kukkucca*)
5. Doubt (*vicikicchā*)

The seven latent tendencies that cause suffering (*anusayas*):

1. Sense desire (*kāmarāga*)
2. The urge to be or become something or someone (*bhavarāga*)

---

3 The four taints or influxes are also called the four floods (*ogha*) or the four bonds (*yoga*).
4 Hindrances to the realisation of deeper happiness.

3. Aggression, anger, hatred (*paṭigha*)
4. Pride, arrogance (*māna*)
5. Mistaken view, misunderstanding (*diṭṭhi*)
6. Doubt, uncertainty (*vicikicchā*)
7. Ignorance (*avijjā*)

The ten impurities or defilements of the mind (*kilesa*s):

1. Desire and attachment (*lobha*)
2. Hatred (*dosa*)
3. Ignorance or lack of understanding of reality, delusion, confusion (*moha*)
4. Pride and self-righteousness (*māna*)
5. Wrong view of reality (*diṭṭhi*)
6. Sceptical doubt, uncertainty (*vicikicchā*)
7. Drowsiness and dullness (*thīna*)
8. Restlessness (*uddhacca*)
9. Absence of moral shame (*ahirika*)
10. Absence of moral fear (*anottappa*)

The ten fetters that bind us to existence (*samyojana*s):

1. Sense desire (*kāmarāga*)
2. Attachment with regard to *jhāna* and its fruits (*bhavarāga*)
3. Hatred (*paṭigha*)
4. Pride, conceit (*māna*)
5. Mistaken view (*diṭṭhi*)
6. Unrealistic belief in rites and rituals (*sīlabbataparāmāsa*)
7. Doubt, scepticism (*vicikicchā*)
8. Jealousy (*issā*)
9. Miserliness (*macchariya*)
10. Misunderstanding, delusion, ignorance (*avijjā*)

Lists of factors that are wholesome and the causes of happiness

The Four Noble Abodes (*brahmavihāras*):

1. Loving kindness (*mettā*)
2. Compassion (*karunā*
3. Sympathetic joy (*muditā*)
4. Equanimity (*upekkhā*)

The seven processes of purification (*visuddhi*):

1. Purification of and through virtue (*sīla-visuddhi*)
2. Purification of consciousness (*citta-visuddhi*)
3. Purification of the idea of 'self' (*diṭṭhi-visuddhi*)
4. Purification by transcending or overcoming doubt (*kankhāvitarana-visuddhi*)
5. Purification by knowledge and vision of what is the path and what not (*maggāmagga-ñāṇadassana-visuddhi*)
6. Purification by knowledge and vision of the way (*paṭipadā-ñāṇadassana-visuddhi*)
7. Purification by knowledge and insight (*ñāṇadassana-visuddhi*)

The ten perfections of mind (*pārami*):

1. Generosity (*dāna*)
2. Virtue (*sīla*)
3. Renunciation or restraint (*nekkhamma*)
4. Wisdom (*paññā*)
5. Diligence, determination, effort (*viriya*)
6. Patience (*khanti*)
7. Truthfulness (*sacca*)
8. Perseverance (*adhiṭṭhāna*)

9.   Loving kindness (*mettā*)
10. Equanimity (*upekkhā*)

Lists of factors that lead to liberation

This category includes the thirty-seven requisites for enlightenment (*bodhipakkhiyadhammā*). These factors develop through the
practice of insight meditation, and together they lead to the happiness of liberating insight.

The four areas or fields where mindfulness can be established
(*satipaṭṭhāna*s):

1.   The body (*kāyānupassanā*)
2.   Feelings (*vedanānupassanā*)
3.   Consciousness (*cittānupassanā*)
4.   All (other) objects that can be observed (*dhammānupassanā*)

The four supreme efforts[5] (*sammappadhānā*):

1.   To remove unwholesome states of mind
2.   To prevent unwholesome states of mind from arising
3.   To develop wholesome states of mind
4.   To cultivate wholesome states of mind that have already
     arisen

The four means of accomplishment (*iddhipāda*):

1.   Wholesome wish (*chanda*)

---

5   These four supreme efforts are aspects of right effort, the sixth factor of the
Eightfold Path.

2. Effort or energy (*viriya*)
3. Consciousness (*citta*)
4. Investigation (*vīmamsa*)

The five controlling faculties (*indriyas*):

1. Confidence (*saddhā*)
2. Effort (*viriya*)
3. Mindfulness (*sati*)
4. Concentration (*samādhi*)
5. Wisdom (*paññā*)

The five powers[6] (*balas*):

1. Confidence (*saddhā*)
2. Effort (*viriya*)
3. Mindfulness (*sati*)
4. Concentration (*samādhi*)
5. Wisdom (*paññā*)

The seven factors of awakening (*bojjhangas*):

1. Mindfulness (*sati*)
2. Investigation of reality (*dhammavicaya*)
3. Effort or energy (*viriya*)
4. Joy or rapture (*pīti*)
5. Serenity or tranquillity of mind (*passaddhi*)
6. Concentration (*samādhi*)
7. Equanimity (*upekkhā*)

---

6   The five powers are in fact the five controlling faculties; when these have been strongly developed they are called powers.

The eight factors of the Eightfold Path that leads to the cessation of suffering (*attha maggangāni*):

1. Right understanding (*sammā-diṭṭhi*)
2. Right thought (*sammā-sankappa*)
3. Right speech (*sammā-vācā*)
4. Right action (*sammā-kammanta*)
5. Right livelihood (*sammā-ājīva*)
6. Right effort (*sammā-vāyāma*)
7. Right mindfulness (*sammā-sati*)
8. Right concentration (*sammā-samādhi*)

GLOSSARY

Abhidhamma: literally 'higher doctrine'; one of the three parts of the *Theravāda Tipiṭaka*, namely the texts that are specifically concerned with Buddhist phenomenology)

Adhimokkha: decision

Adhiṭṭhāna: determination

Adosa: the absence of hatred; benevolence

Āhāra: source of matter (see appendix 1)

Ahāra: nutriment

Ahetuka: rootless; designation of eighteen specific types of consciousness

Ahetuka-citta: rootless consciousness

Ahirika: shamelessness

Ākāsadhāthu: interatomic space

Ākāsadhātu: space element

Ākāsanañcāyatana-viññāṇa: consciousness with 'infinite space' as object; consciousness that experiences the first formless absorption consciousness

Ākiñcaññāyatana-viññāṇa: consciousness with 'nothingness' as object; consciousness that experiences the third formless absorption consciousness

Akusala: unwholesome, not leading to happiness and wisdom

Alobha: absence of desire; generosity

Amoha: absence of ignorance; synonym for wisdom

Anāgāmi: literally 'non-returner', indicating someone who has realised the third stage of enlightenment

Anāgāmī: non-returner; he/she who has attained the third degree of enlightenment

Anattā: egolessness, no-self, uncontrollability, ungovernability, unpredictability

Anguttara Nikāya: literally, 'Gradual Sayings' or 'Numerical Discourses'; a Buddhist scripture, the fourth of the five *nikāya*s or collections in the Sutta Pitaka, which is one of the 'three baskets' that comprise the Pali Tipitaka of Theravada Buddhism

Anicca: impermanence, changeability

Animitta: formlessness, signlessness, designation of *nibbāna*

*Aññasamāna-cetasika*s: mental factors that can work together with both wholesome and unwholesome types of consciousness; designation of the first thirteen mental factors

Anottappa: lack of scruples, moral fearlessness

Anupādisesa-nibbāna: literally, 'Enlightenment without a residue'; description of the realisation of an *arahat* at his death, where all mental and physical experiences come to an end

Anusaya: latent impurity of mind, causing suffering

Āpattipatti-avijjā: ignorance that has the nature of not clearly understanding what is happening in the moment

Āpodhātu: the water element

Appamaññā: illimitable; compassion and sympathetic joy are the two illimitables mentioned

Appanā-samādhi: the level of concentration that is called absorption concentration

Appaṇihita: freedom from desire; one of the three characteristics of enlightenment

Arahat: literally 'purified one', indicating someone who has realised the fourth and final stage of enlightenment, in which the impurities of mind have been completely eradicated

Ariyasaccāni: Noble Truths; description of the Four Noble Truths

Arūpa-jhāna: immaterial state of absorption

Asaññasattā-bhūmi: a fine-material realm, where there are no mental processes at all; there is only a temporary fine-material form

Asankhata: the unconditioned, a designation for enlightenment

Āsava: the four taints or influxes

Asura: jealous demigod, symbol of the realm of jealousy

Atita-bhavaṅga: the passive mental state, when no object is received

Attā: 'self', soul or ego

Attha maggangāni: the eight factors of the Eightfold Path that leads to the cessation of suffering

Atthasālinī: a well-known commentary on the first book of the *Abhidhamma Piṭaka*, the *Dhammasanganī*, written by the Venerable Bhadantācariya Buddhaghosa

Attavādupādāna: clinging to the notion that there is a self

Āvajjana: adverting to an object; one of the functions that can be performed by consciousness

Avijjā: ignorance, misunderstanding, delusion, unconsciousness regarding what is happening in or to us here and now

Ayoniso-manasikāra: unwise or unskilfull attention

Bala: (potential) power, meaning the five *indriya*s at a deeper level

Bardo: a phase between death consciousness and the next rebirth consicousness that can last up to a maximum of forty-nine days; taught in the Tibetan schools of Buddhism that developed later

Bhava: becoming, the tenth link in chain of dependent origination

Bhāvanā: development, growth, meditation

Bhāvanā-saddhā: faith or confidence that is based on the experience of the fruits of meditation

Bhavaṅga: basic undercurrent of consciousness, 'stream of consciousness'. It concerns one of the functions of consciousness. It is difficult to find an exact translation of this 'dream state' which does not only take place at night but also in the daytime, in between all the stimuli we experience. In English this function of consciousness is often translated as 'life-continuum'

Bhavaṅga-sota: the stream of life-continuum

Bhavaṅgupaccheda: the moment in cognitive processes where the passive state is disrupted

Bhavarāga: the urge to be or become something or someone

Bhāvarūpa: physical aspect of masculinity or femininity

Bhavāsava: the desire to be or to become; one of the four taints or influxes

Bhavatanhā: urge to be or become somebody or something (literally: craving for existence)

Bhikkhu: Buddhist monk

Bhikkhuni: Buddhist nun

Bodhipakkhiyadhammā: requisites for enlightenment; usually thirty-seven are mentioned

Bodhisattva: someone striving for enlightenment, developing certain perfections of mind, such as generosity, patience and wisdom (Pali: *bodhisatta*)

Bojjhanga: factor of awakening; usually seven are mentioned

Brahmavihāras: sublime states of mind or Noble Abodes (see appendix 1)

Buddha: title for someone who has awakened from ignorance or delusion

Byāpāda: aversion, resistance; one of the five hindrances (*nīvaranas*)

Calana-bhavanga: the moment in cognitive processes where the first impulse takes place in the passive state of mind

Cetanā: intention, volition

Cetasika: mental factor or concomitant. There are fifty-two mental factors; they are the second ultimate reality

Chanda: wish, wish to do

Citta: type of consciousness. There are one hundred and twenty-one types of consciousness; they are the first ultimate reality

Cittānupassanā: the third of the four *satipatthānas*, namely mindfulness of mind

Citta-visuddhi: purification of consciousness; one of the seven purifications

Cuti-citta: death consciousness

Dāna: generosity

Deva: divine being, living in the realm of sensual bliss

Dhamma: the teachings of the Buddha

Dhamma: natural phenomenon, mental object, a state, truth, reality, wisdom, action, skilful action or practice

Dhammacchanda: the desire or wish for deeper wisdom

Dhammānupassanā: the last of the four *satipaṭṭhāna*s, namely mindfulness of mental and physical phenomena in general. Those specifically mentioned in this context are: the five hindrances, the five aggregates or aspects of clinging, the six inner and outer sense bases, the seven factors of awakening, and the Four Noble Truths

Dhammapada: well-known Buddhist text with aphorisms and verses of wisdom

Dhammasanganī: literally, 'Enumeration of Phenomena'; one of the seven books of the *Abhidhamma Piṭaka*

Dhamma-vicaya: intuitive investigation of phenomena; one of the synonyms for wisdom

Dhātu: basic element; the four basic elements are earth, water, fire and air

Dhātukathā: literally 'Discourse on Elements', one of the seven books of the *Abhidhamma Piṭaka*

Diṭṭhāsava: the influx of wrong view; one of the four taints or influxes

Diṭṭhi: wrong view

Diṭṭhi-visuddhi: purification of the idea of 'self'; one of the seven purifications

Diṭṭhupādāna: clinging to wrong views; one of the four forms of attachment or clinging

Domanassa-vedanā: mental unpleasant feeling

Dosa: hatred, aversion

Dukkha: the most conventional translation is 'suffering'; the most accurate translation is 'unsatisfactoriness'. Other renderings are pain, conflict, frustration, instability, insecurity, burden or vulnerability

Dukkha-sacca: the first Noble Truth, the 'truth that there is suffering'

Dukkha-vedanā: physical unpleasant feeling

Dvāra: door or gateway to (six forms of) sense perception

Ekaggatā: concentration or one-pointedness

Gati-nimitta: an image or vision of a future life (see chapter 5)

Gocararūpa: the sense fields of colour and light, sound, smell and taste

Hadayarūpa: the physical heart-base

Hasituppāda-citta: smile-producing-consciousness; the smile of an *arahat*

Hetu: driving force for wholesome or unwholesome *kamma* (see chapter 14)

Hiri: shame

Iddhipāda: means of accomplishment; four means are usually mentioned

Indriya: wholesome power or factor that is developed by means of insight meditation; literally, controlling faculty (see appendix 1)

Issa: jealousy or envy

Issā: envy, jealousy

Jarā: old age

Jāti: birth

Javana: mental scanning, one of the functions of consciousness

Javana-citta: mentally scanning type of consciousness

Jhāna: deep level of absorption or concentration

Jhāna-citta: fine-material or immaterial type of consciousness that can be experienced through the practice of tranquillity meditation

Jīvitindriya: physical or mental vitality

Kabaḷīkārāhāra: nutriment

Kāmacchanda: sense pleasure and desire

Kāmarāga: sense desire

Kāmāsava: sensual desire; one of the four taints or influxes

Kāmatanhā: sense desire

Kāmāvacara: in the sphere of the senses; designation of ordinary consciousness

Kāmāvacara-kriyā-citta: functional wholesome type of consciousness that are experienced by arahats

Kāmāvacara-kusala-citta: a 'beautiful' type of consciousness that arises when we create wholesome kamma

Kamma: the law of cause and effect

Kammabhava: becoming, which refers to the active behavioural patterns in speech, action and thought

Kamma-nimitta: object perceived with the senses that is related to a previous action (see chapter 4)

Kammaññatā: wieldiness

Kammassakatā-sammā-diṭṭhi: right view as regards the processes of cause and effect

Kāmupādāna: clinging to sensual pleasure; one of the four forms of attachment or clinging

Kankhāvitarana-visuddhi: purification by overcoming doubt; one of the seven purifications

Karunā: compassion

Kasina: object or device that is used as an object for concentration when practising tranquillity meditation

Kathāvatthu: literally, 'Points of Controversy'; one of the seven books of the Abhidhamma Piṭaka

Kāyānupassanā: the first of the four *satipaṭṭhāna*s, namely mindfulness of the body

Khandha: constituent of human existence; five constituents are usually mentioned

Khanika-samādhi: level of concentration that is called 'moment concentration'; the practice of insight meditation develops this form of concentration in particular

Khanika-vimutti: momentary liberation

Khanti: patience, tolerance; one of the ten perfections of mind

Khema: state of security, safety and stability; this term is used to describe enlightenment

Kilesa: impurity, taint or defilement of the mind (see appendix 1)

Kriyā: functional

Kriyā-citta: functional types of consciousness that arise in *arahats* instead of the universal wholesome types of consciousness

Kukkucca: guilt or remorse

Kusala: wholesome

Lahutā: lightness

Lakkhaṇarūpa: stages of material phenomena: arising, presence and growth, decay and dissolution

Lobha: desire

Loka: realm or sphere of consciousness

Lokapala: protector of the world; usually two are mentioned, moral shame and fear of wrongdoing

Lokiya: mundane

Lokuttara: supramundane; designation of the types of consciousness that are related to the experience of enlightenment

Macchariya: avarice, miserliness

Magga: path

Magga-citta: path-consciousness

Maggāmagga-ñāṇadassana-visuddhi: purification by knowledge and vision of what is the path and what not; one of the seven purifications

Magga-sacca: the fourth Noble Truth, the 'truth of the way leading to the cessation of suffering, namely the eightfold path' (see appendix 1)

Mahā: great

Mahaggata: sublime

Mahaggata-citta: designation for the (twenty-seven fine-material and immaterial) types of consciousness that are related to the practice of tranquillity meditation

Mahāyāna: literally 'great vehicle'; a school of Buddhism that developed later

Māna: pride, conceit

Manasikāra: attention

Manodvāravajjana-citta: consciousness that adverts to the mind-door

Manodvārāvajjana-citta:

Mantra: sound, word or phrase as object of meditation

Marana: dying, death

Mātika: schedules which are used to define and classify all kinds of psychological and philosophical ideas; these schedules serve as the framework for the whole Abhidhamma

Mettā: loving kindness

Mettā-bhāvanā: the cultivation or practice of loving kindness

Micchā-diṭṭhi: wrong view

Micchāpattipatti-avijjā: ignorance that wrongly interprets the reality of the moment

Middha: sluggishness or inertia of the mental factors

Moha: ignorance, delusion

Muditā: sympathetic joy

Mudutā: malleability

Nāma: name, mind

Nāma-rūpa: name and form; mind and matter

Ñāna: intuitive wisdom or insight

Ñāṇadassana-visuddhi: purification by knowledge and insight; one of the seven purifications

Nekkhamma: renunciation, restraint

N'evasaññā-n'āsaññāyatana-viññāṇa: consciousness of 'the sphere where there is neither perception nor non-perception'; consciousness that experiences the fourth formless absorption consciousness

Nibbāna: literally 'not or no longer blowing or burning'; this term is used to indicate the state of enlightenment

Nirodha: cessation

Nirodha-sacca: the third Noble Truth, the 'truth of the cessation of suffering'; this truth is realised through the experience of *nibbāna*

Nīvaraṇa: afflictive emotion; literally, hindrance (see appendix 1)

Ottappa: fear or moral wrongdoing

Paccayadhammā: *Abhidhamma*-theory concerning twenty-four conditions

Pāguññatā: skilfulness, proficiency

Pakati-saddhā: basic confidence or faith in performing wholesome deeds like generosity, ethically appropriate behaviour and patience

Pakiṇṇakā-cetasika: occasional mental factors that can accompany wholesome as well as unwholesome types of consciousness

Pali: the language used in the oldest Buddhist scriptures

Pañcadvāravajjana-citta: consciousness that is adverting to (one of) the five sense-doors

Pañcakkhandhā: the five aggregates of constituents of life

Pañcaviññāṇa-citta: sense-consciousness

Paññā: wisdom, liberating insight

Papañcas: proliferations; designation of desire, wrong view and conceit

Pārami: perfection of mind (see appendix 1)

Pasādarūpa: the five senses

Passaddhi: serenity

Paṭhavīdhātu: earth element

Paṭiccasamuppāda: the chain or cycle of dependent origination

Paṭigha: hatred, anger

Paṭipadā-ñāṇadassana-visuddhi:

Paṭisandhi-citta: rebirth consciousness

Patthāna: literally 'Book of Conditional Relations'; one of the seven books of the *Abhidhamma Piṭaka*

Peta: hungry ghost, symbol for the realm of unfulfilled desire
    (Sanskrit: *preta*)

Phala: fruition

Phala-citta: fruition-consciousness

Phala-samāpatti: the skill of experienced meditators of being able
    to repeatedly experience the supramundane fruition types of
    consciousness, once they have realised enlightenment

Phassa: contact, sense impression

Piṭaka: literally 'basket'; designation of the three categories of
    scriptures of Theravāda Buddhism

Pīti: rapture, joy

Puggalapaññatti: literally, 'Concepts of Individuals'; one of the
    seven books of the *Abhidhamma Piṭaka*

Rūpa: matter, the body

Sabbacittasādhārana-cetasikas: universal mental factors; these first
    concomitants arise with all types of consciousness.

Sacca: truth

Saddhā: confidence, trust, faith

Sakadāgāmī: literally 'once-returner', indicating someone who has
    realised the second stage of enlightenment

Saḷāyatana: the six senses, as the fifth link in the chain of depen-
    dent origination

Samādhi: meditation; concentration or one-pointedness of mind
    (see appendix 1)

Samanera: Buddhist novice or student-monk

Samatha: tranquillity, calm, relaxation

Samatha-bhāvanā: tranquillity meditation (literally, 'the cultivation
    of tranquillity')

Sammā: right or correct; often used as in accordance with the aim
    of following the Eightfold Path

Sammappadhānā: designation of the four supreme efforts

Sammā-ājīva: right livelihood, one of the factors of the Eightfold
    Path

Sammā-diṭṭhi: right view, one of the factors of the Eightfold Path

Sammā-kammanta: right action, one of the factors of the Eightfold Path

Sammā-samādhi: right concentration, one of the factors of the Eightfold Path

Sammā-sankappa: right thought, one of the factors of the Eightfold Path

Sammā-sati: right mindfulness, one of the factors of the Eightfold Path

Sammā-vācā: right speech, one of the factors of the Eightfold Path

Sammā-vāyāma: right effort or dedication, one of the factors of the Eightfold Path

Sammohavinodanī: title of an important commentary in *Theravāda* Buddhism

Samuccheda-vimutti: complete liberation

Sampaṭicchana: receiving, one of the functions of consciousness

Sampaṭicchana-citta: consciousness in a cognitive process that clearly receives an object

Sampayoganaya: analysis where one investigates with which types of consciousness the various mental factors can associate

Samsāra: cycle of birth and rebirth, also called the wheel of life

Samudaya-sacca: the second Noble Truth, the 'truth that there is a cause of suffering, namely desire'

Samvega-vatthu: object or sign that evokes a sense of spiritual urgency

Samyojana: constricting driving force, 'fetter' binding us to existence

Sangha: community of monks, nuns and lay followers of the Buddha and the *Dhamma*

Sangahanaya: analysis where one investigates with which mental factors the various types of consciousness can combine

Sankhāra: volitional activities, the second link in the chain of dependent origination

Saññā: cognition, perception

Santi: peace (a description of enlightenment)

Santīrana: investigating, one of the functions of consciousness

Santīrana-citta: consciousness in a cognitive process where a received object is investigated

Sati: mindfulness; 'remembering what is happening in and to us in the present moment'

Satipaṭṭhāna: application of mindfulness, field where mindfulness can be cultivated (see appendix 1)

Sa-upādisesa-nibbāna: enlightenment with a residue; designation of an *arahat*

Sīla: morality, virtue, ethics, discipline

Sīlabbataparāmāsa: unrealistic belief in rites and rituals; one of the ten fetters

Sīlabbatupādāna: clinging to rites and rituals; one of the four forms of attachment

Sīla-visuddhi: purification of and through virtue; one of the seven purifications

Sobhana-citta: designation of the twenty-four wholesome types of consciousness; literally, beautiful consciousness

Sobhana-sādharana-cetasikas: universal wholesome mental factors

Somanassa-vedanā: mental pleasant feeling

Sotāpanna: literally 'streamwinner', a description of someone who has realised the first stage of enlightenment

Sotāpatti: of or by a streamwinner

Sotāpatti-magga: path consciousness of (or to be) a streamwinner

Suddhāvāsa: designation of the five 'Pure Abodes' or highest fine-material realms

Sukha-vedanā: physical pleasant feeling

Suññattā: emptiness, voidness, a characteristic of enlightenment

Sutta: teaching or discourse of the Buddha

Tadārammana: registering, one of the functions of consciousness

Tadālambana-citta: registering-consciousness; synonym for *tadārammaṇa-citta*

Tadārammaṇa-citta: registering-consciousness

Taṇhā: desire, craving

Tatramajjhattatā: equanimity; literally, there in the middle

Tāvatiṃsa: one of the heavenly realms

Tejodhātu: fire element

Theravāda: literally, 'advice of the elders', indicating the original form of Buddhism. Nowadays this tradition is prevalent in Southeast Asia and in Sri Lanka. *Mahāyāna* and Tibetan Buddhism emerged from *Theravāda*

Tilakkhaṇa: the three universal characteristics of existence, namely impermanence, unsatisfactoriness and uncontrollability

Tipiṭaka: literally 'the three baskets'. It indicates the Buddhist scriptures, comprising of three divisions, namely the *Vinaya*, the *Sutta*s and the *Abhidhamma*

Thīna: dullness of consciousness

Thīna-middha: dullness and sluggishness. One of the five hindrances (*nīvaraṇas*)

Uddhacca: restlessness, agitation

Uddhacca-kukkucca: restlessness and remorse

Ummattaka: the state of madness, having lost one's senses or being very disturbed

Upacāra-samādhi: level of concentration that is called access concentration

Upādāna: clinging, attachment, the ninth link in the chain of dependent origination

Upapattibhava: the result of active behavioural patterns, taking place in the future

Upekkhā: equanimity; one of the Four Noble Abodes

Upekkhā-vedanā: neutral mental feeling

Utu: temperature; climate factors and organic factors

Vajrayāna: literally, 'the diamond vehicle', indicating a later form of Buddhism, popularly known as Tibetan Buddhism

Vājodhātu: the air element

Vatta: three rounds in the chain of dependent arising

Vāyodhātu: the air element; one of the four basic elements

Vedanā: feeling

Vedanānupassanā: the second of the four bases *satipaṭṭhāna*s, namely mindfulness of feelings

Vibhanga: literally, 'Book of Analysis'; one of the seven books of the *Abhidhamma Piṭaka*

Vibhavatanhā: urge to destroy

Vicāra: sustained application, deliberation

Vicikicchā: doubt, scepticism

Vikārarūpa: changeability of matter

Vikkhambhana-vimutti: long-term liberation

Vīmamsa: investigation (synonym for wisdom); one of the four means of accomplishment

Vimutti: liberation (a description of enlightenment)

Vinaya: morality, ethics; one of the three parts of the *Tipiṭaka*

Viññāṇa: consciousness; also used specifically as rebirth linking consciousness in the model of dependent origination

Viññāṇanañcāyatana-viññāṇa: consciousness with 'infinite consciousness' as its object; consciousness that experiences the second formless absorption consciousness

Viññattirūpa: bodily and verbal expression

Vipāka: result, effect, the fruit of pervious *kamma*

Vipāka-citta: resultant consciousness

Vipassanā: insight, liberating insight, wisdom, intuitive understanding of reality as it is

Vipassanā-bhāvanā: insight meditation (literally 'the cultivation of insight')

Virati: abstinence, renunciation

Viriya: diligence, determination, effort, energy, dedication

Visuddhi: process of purification that happens through the practice of insight meditation (see appendix 1)

Visuddhimagga: The Path of Purification, written in c. 400 CE by a Sinhalese monk, Venerable Bhadantācariya Buddhaghosa, and translated into English by Bhikkhu Ñānamoli under the title *The Path of Purification*. The book is one of the most detailed handbooks of Buddhist meditation, as well as an important commentary on original Buddhist texts

Vitakka: initial application, coupling

Votthapana: determining, one of the functions of consciousness

Votthapana-citta: consciousness that determines an object in a cognitive process

Yamaka: literally, 'Book of Pairs'; one of the seven books of the *Abhidhamma Piṭaka*

Yoniso-manasikāra: wise attention

RECOMMENDED READING

Books

Anālayo, Venerable. *Satipaṭṭhāna*. Birmingham: Windhorse Publications, 2003.

Bodhi, Bhikkhu. *A Comprehensive Manual of Abhidhamma*. Kandy: Buddhist Publication Society, 1993.

Epstein, Mark. *Thoughts without a Thinker: Psychotherapy from a Buddhist Perspective*. New York: Basic Books, 1995.

———. *Going to Pieces without Falling Apart: A Buddhist Perspective on Wholeness*. New York: Broadway Books, 1998.

Goldstein, Joseph. *Insight Meditation: The Practice of Freedom*. Boston: Shambhala Publications, 1993.

———. *Mindfulness: A Practical Guide to Awakening*. Boulder, Colorado: Sounds True, 2013.

———, and Jack Kornfield. *Seeking the Heart of Wisdom: The Path of Insight Meditation*. Boston: Shambhala Publications, 1987.

Goleman, Daniel. *Destructive Emotions: A Scientific Dialogue with the Dalai Lama*. New York: Bantam Books, 2003.

Gorkom, Nina van. *Abhidhamma in Daily Life*. Colombo: Gunasekera Trust.

Kabat-Zinn, Jon. *Full Catastrophe Living: Using the Wisdom of Your Body and Mind to Face Stress, Pain, and Illness*. New York: Dell Publishing, 1990.

———. *Wherever You Go, There You Are: Mindfulness Meditation in Everyday Life*. New York: Hyperion, 1994.

Kornfield, Jack. *A Path with Heart: A Guide Through the Perils and Promises of Spiritual Life*. New York: Bantam Books, 1993.

————. *After the Ecstasy, the Laundry: How the Heart Grows Wise on the Spiritual Path.* New York: Bantam Books, 2000.

Koster, Frits. *Liberating Insight: Introduction to Buddhist Psychology and Insight Meditation.* Chiang Mai: Silkworm Books, 2004.

————. *Buddhist Meditation in Stress Management.* Chiang Mai: Silkworm Books, 2007.

Ledi, Sayadaw. *The Manuals of Buddhism.* Rangoon: Department of Religious Affairs, 1981.

Mendis. *The Abhidhamma in Practice.* Kandy: Buddhist Publication Society, 1985.

Ñānamoli. *Visuddhimagga, the Path of Purification.* Kandy: Buddhist Publication Society, 1956.

Narada. *A Manual of Abhidhamma.* Rangoon: Department of Religious Affairs, 1956.

————. *Teachings of the Buddha.* Kandy: Buddhist Publication Society, 1988.

Nyānaponika Thera. *Abhidhamma Studies.* Boston: Wisdom Publications, 1949.

————. *The Heart of Buddhist Meditation.* Kandy: Buddhist Publication Society, 1954.

Nyanatiloka, Venerable. *Buddhist Dictionary: A Manual of Buddhist Terms and Doctrines.* Chiang Mai: Silkworm Books, 2007.

Rahula, Walpola. *What the Buddha taught.* New York: Grove Press, 1959.

Salzberg, Sharon. *Lovingkindness: The Revolutionary Art of Happiness.* Boston: Shambhala Publications, 1995.

Sayadaw, U Pandita. *In this very life: The liberation teachings of the Buddha.* Boston: Wisdom Publications, 1992.

————. *On the Path of Freedom: A mind of wise discernment and openness,* Malaysia: Buddhist Wisdom Centre, 1995.

Sīlananda, U. *The Four Foundations of Mindfulness.* Boston: Wisdom Publications, 1990.

Sircar, Rina. *The Psycho-ethical Aspects of Abhidhamma*. Lanham: University Press of America, 1984.

Trungpa, Chögyam. *Glimpses of Abhidharma*. Boston: Shambhala Publications.

Van den Brink, Erik, and Frits Koster. *Mindfulness-Based Compassionate Living*. Routledge, 2015.

Yupho, Dhanit. *Vipassanā Bhāvanā*. Bangkok: Phra Dhammakkhanda Foundation, 1988.

Forums

There is a discussion forum for anyone who is interested in the *Tipiṭaka* and in *Abhidhamma* study. The forum has been in existence for more than thirty years under the auspices of Thai teacher Khun Sujin Boriharnwanaket. See http://groups.yahoo.com/group/dhammastudygroup/

Informative websites

www.abhidhamma.org
www.compassionateliving.info
www.dharma.org
www.fritskoster.com
www.gaiahouse.co.uk
www.metta.org
www.passaddhi.com
www.satipanya.org.uk
www.spiritrock.org
www.vipassana.ie
www.vipassanametta.org

ABOUT THE AUTHOR

 Frits Koster (1957) is a Vipassana meditation teacher and a certified teacher of Mindfulness-Based Stress Reduction (MBSR) and Mindfulness-Based Cognitive Therapy (MBCT). He has also trained and worked as a psychiatric nurse. He has taught mindfulness in mental health settings, including clinics and hospitals, for many years.

He has been practicing Theravada Buddhism for more than thirty years and was a Buddhist monk for six years in the 1980s. During the period he was a monk he studied Buddhist psychology at various monasteries in Southeast Asia. He is a member of the faculty of the Institute for Mindfulness-Based Approaches (IMA) and the Institute for Mindfulness (IvM) in the Netherlands, as well as various training institutes across Europe.

Frits is the author of several books (Asoka, Boom). Some of these books have been translated into English, including *Liberating Insight* (Silkworm Books, 2004) and *Buddhist Meditation in Stress Management* (Silkworm Books, 2007). He is co-author, with Erik van den Brink, of *Mindfulness-Based Compassionate Living* (published in Dutch, German and English). See www.fritskoster.com and www.compassionateliving.info.